Adoption
Is a Family Affair!

What Relatives and Friends *Must* Know

Adoption
Is a Family Affair!

What Relatives and Friends *Must* Know

Patricia Irwin Johnston

Perspectives Press, Inc.
Indianapolis, Indiana

Adoption Is a Family Affair! is dedicated to the members of the Adoption Waiting Room on-line community. Profits from its sale will be shared with INCIID on their behalf.

Perspectives Press, Inc.
P.O. Box 90318
Indianapolis, IN 46290-0318
USA
(317)872-3055
http://www.perspectivespress.com

Cover and interior design by Bookwrights
Manufactured in the United States of America

Library of Congress Cataloging in publication data:
Johnston, Patricia Irwin.
    Adoption is a family affair! : what relatives and friends must know / Patricia
    Irwin Johnston.
        p. cm.
    Includes bibliographical references.
    ISBN 0-944934-28-5 (pbk.)
        1. Adoption. 2. Adoption—Psychological aspects. I. Title.
    HV875 .J676 2001
    362.73'4—dc21   2001021301

Acknowledgments

This book came about because the participants in the online Adoption Waiting Room which I moderate for the International Council on Infertility Information Dissemination felt it was urgently needed. I had thought so, too, for quite some time, and, as the publisher at Perspectives Press I had encouraged several authors who had come to me with the idea for such a book. No manuscript ever materialized.

The INCIIDers and I took matters into our own hands. We brainstormed on line at http://www.inciid.org/forums/adoption_waiting/index.html on and off over several weeks about what topics belonged in the table of contents for this book. Participants shared anecdotes that found their way inside these pages. We talked about possible titles. Eventually this small book was developed to fill the need these waiting parents had for something to share with their friends and families to help them "get with the program" of bringing a child into the family by adoption.

Though I edit the work of others daily, it's just about as bad an idea to try to be one's own editor as it is to try to be one's own physician or attorney! I depended on my long suffering good friend the versatile Cynthia V. N. Peck, retired teacher, social worker, author (*Parents at Last!* and *Adoption Today*), magazine editor (*Fostering Families Today*) and publisher (*Roots & Wings*) as well as single mom extraordinaire to a glorious grown up brood to be my editor. Cindy pared me down, moved me around, and brought me up to speed with great patience and a good dose of punch and pizzazz. Thanks, Cyn!

I'd like to thank my own extended family—my parents and Dave's, our siblings and aunts and uncles—for not needing such a book in their time. On Dave's side of the family, adoption was already firmly entrenched and understood. His parents and one of his aunts and uncles adopted all of their children, so that his generation of cousins included four by adoption and two by birth. My family had not experienced adoption before, but they embraced it with absolutely no reservations from the beginning. There has been a stumble or two along the way, but the Johnstons and the Irwins have dusted themselves off quite well, thank you! Thanks to these two wonderful wide families, our kids have always "belonged" in every way.

Table of Contents

The Announcement

Melika and Ahmad and Nancy and Fred are two couples I know well. Both families have been hoping for a child for years, and they've been working actively on that. Melika and Ahmad have gotten pregnant several times, but they've been unable to carry a pregnancy to term. Nancy and Fred have never been pregnant, despite medications and invasive procedures.

Margaret is a member of my church, 35 and single and childless, despite the fact that she'd like to have found a partner and married and had babies by now. Sam and Stewart are gay and have lived together in a committed relationship for ten years. For both Marcia and Erv, who are in their late 40s, theirs is a second marriage. Erv has nearly grown children from his first marriage, but Marcia had no children. Ruben and Anita have given birth to three healthy children but have room in their hearts and their home for more.

What these folks have in common is that the reaction of their families to their decision to adopt a child has surprised and disappointed them. They expected joy! They expected support! What they got (at least what they feel they heard) was shock and fear and apparent disapproval.

"Oh, no, honey. Why would you want to do *that*?" followed by "Just keep trying, you'll get pregnant again." or

"I read about this great doctor over in Big City. Have you thought about seeing him?" or

"But you're not married! Children need two parents. You can't do this alone." or

"You know we love Sam/Stewart, darling, but your life is hard enough. How could you do that to a child?" or

"At your age? You were out of college and Mom and I were almost ready to retire when we were your age! You can't start parenting now!"

"But you have such a lovely family! Why would you want to risk exposing our grandchildren to the dangers of adopting one of *those* kids?" or

"Adopting! Why everybody knows that adopted kids have all kinds of problems. What kind of person gives away his own flesh and blood?"

"To be honest, son, I'm not sure I can love somebody else's child."

This is a book for the parents as well as the brothers and sisters and close friends of people like Melika and Ahmad, Nancy and Fred, Sam and Stewart, Marcia and Erv, Ruben and Anita, and Margaret. These would-be adopters love you—their families—and want you to share their joy as they build a family. They know that it's hard for you to understand something you've not experienced before. They understand that adoption is not something that most people think of as a "first choice" route to parenthood. With this book they are hoping that you'll get the facts, learn what you need to know, and deal with your fears and reservations so that you can embrace their decision wholeheartedly and make the leap of faith that they have made into a whole new world. This is a world, after all, that is going to include your loved one's children. With you or without you, these children will arrive, and they are coming through adoption.

A word of explanation: most of the time this book will appear to "speak to" the adopters' parents (a.k.a. grandparents-to-be). I've written that way for the sake of simplicity. What sounds as if it is being written only to the parents of prospective adopters is meant just as fully for the brothers and sisters and good friends and co-workers of those same adopters. My own experience and the experience of literally thousands of adopters I've known in the past twenty-five years tells me that "the older generation" has no corner on snafus, blunders, misunderstandings, and outright insults when it comes to their interactions with those who build their families by adoption. The problem is not age, but ignorance. Everybody in the family has some learning to do, so let's get to it!

Your Personal, Private Fears

Now that your loved ones have announced their intention to adopt, your mind may be filled with worry. Most of this worry is related to fear of the unknown or fear based on inaccurate information. This can be dealt with. Let's try.

Is Adoption Really Just Long-Term Temporary Care?

You've seen those TV programs and magazine stories about open adoptions and searches and reunions. You may be wondering how "permanent" adoption is, because you don't want to see the heart of someone you care about broken.

Rest assured that adoption *is* permanent. The laws in each state, when followed properly, would insure that there would be no Baby Jessica or Baby Richard cases of children torn years later from the arms of the only parents they have known since birth. The key is following the letter of the law. That takes ethics, research, patience, and the guidance of experienced legal and social service professionals.

In each and every one of the flamboyant cases of reclaimed children covered by the media, the law had not been followed. A birthfather had not been properly identified to the professionals arranging the adoption or he had not been informed of the pregnancy so that his parental rights could be appropriately terminated. A family in a state that disallowed independent adoption tried to adopt in another state and was unfamiliar with that state's laws. These situations can be avoided by recognizing that laws are not made to be broken or avoided but to protect everyone. A service provider who suggests a way to "get around" procedure or law (for example, suggesting that one use an obscure newspaper classified ad to "notify" a birthfather who could be directly contacted) should be avoided at all costs.

Every profession has its "bad apples," practitioners who are less than ethical, those who are not really competent or who don't work to stay abreast of changes in growth and practice, those who are "in it for the money." The very best way for your family's adoption to be "safe" is for the would-be parents to choose their professional advisors carefully. They should check the credentials and the business reputations of all service providers they use—social service or adoption agencies, attorneys, or "facilitators." Adopters can do this by making contacts with consumer protection groups:

• Adopters can check professionals' credentials in several ways. Domestic adoption agencies are licensed by their states and licensure can be verified through the state's department of family and children's services. Ethical, full time adoption attorneys are almost always members of the American Academy of Adoption Attorneys. Agencies practicing in the area of international adoption should be members of the Joint Council on International Children's Services. If the service provider is not affiliated in these ways, ask why.

- Adopters should also call an adoptive parent support group located in the same state (preferably the same city) as the office of the practitioner and ask them about the organization's reputation. They should ask, as well, for the names of group members who have used this practitioner's services and consider speaking directly to these clients.

- Adopters should contact the Better Business Bureau in the city where the practice is located and verify that there have been no complaints. Since few complaints are actually made, any that are on file should be considered as red flags.

- Similarly, each state's Attorney General's office has a Consumer Protection Division where reports of problems are gathered. Be sure that the practitioner is not known as a "problem company" there.

Adoptive parents *are* the "real," definitive parents to their children. We'll talk in more detail about the eccentricities, challenges and benefits of openness in adoption planning and open adoption in a later section. For now, please know that when the birth and adoptive families have been fully prepared and supported, an ongoing open adoption is nothing at all like "shared parenting" after a divorce. Adoptive parents are always the legal, moral, and psychological parents to their children. Birthparents cannot (and most would not want to) interfere in or influence the day-to-day decisions about discipline, education, religious training, etc. that all parents make for their children.

Adoption *is* lifelong. Despite the stories that you have heard, all reliable research on adoption demonstrates that the overwhelming majority of adopted people feel fully connected to, loved by, and bonded with their adoptive families. But at the same time, many adopted people who were not brought up in open adoptions have had to address their curiosity through fantasy about the mysterious unknown. This may lead to a strong need to have more direct and concrete information about their birthfamilies. Some say that they want medical information, or explanations for some personality and physical traits that are clearly genetically-based. They may wonder if these genetic connections might lead to a better "psychological fit." But the need to search hardly springs from idle curiosity. In a culture in which adoption is seen as being "second best" by large segments of society and even some of their own family members (more on the concept of anti-adoption bias and *adoptism* later), it makes perfect sense that many adopted people feel drawn to figure this all out for themselves. They may wonder about the emotional connections that occur between genetic relatives and whether those can be stronger than connections with the family in which they grew up. When they do make a connection with birthrelatives, the vast majority of people who were adopted are able to build cordial and comfortable and important relationships with extended birthfamily members, but at the same time nearly all of them feel emphatically that their adopted family is their warm, safe core—their "real" family, if you will.

📖 Learn more about it:

An Adopted Woman by Katrina Maxtone Graham (Remi Books, 1981)

Searching for a Past: The Adopted Adult's Unique Process of Finding Identity by Jayne E. Schooler (Pinon Press, 1995)

The Children of Open Adoption by Kathleen Silber and Patricia Martinez Dorner (Corona Publications, 1994)

The American Adoption Congress
http://www.americanadoptioncongress.org

Bonding

The main thing that is required in order for two healthy people to begin the dance of attachment with one another is for them to be open to the opportunity to trust one another. Healthy newborns are primed to attach. Children who have been in a single loving foster home and have attached to their fosterparents can, with loving support, transfer that attachment to their new families.

Attachment, or bonding, is a relationship between two human beings extending through time and place and based upon their mutual ability to trust each other to meet one another's needs. Bonding has been a hot topic in the world of childbirth for many years, driving the trends that resulted in various approaches to prepared childbirth, fathers (and siblings and grandparents) in the delivery room, and a variety of delivery environments from home to birthing chairs to suites to pools, etc. Some people assume that a "perfect birth" experience can provide a kind of "super glue" experience tying family members to one another. But birthing experiences and genes are not what tie most closely-connected people together.

It's true that we first learn to attach to other humans as babies. Mothers (and fathers) begin to attach to their coming children during the pregnancy experience. We know that a baby hears and grows attuned to his mother's voice in utero and can instinctively recognize her body's fragrance within hours of birth. Babies are born open to and eager to bond to the one who cares for and loves them during their vulnerable first hours and days and weeks. When babies express their needs (for food, for warmth, for dry diapers, for cuddling) to a parent who, over the course of any day, responds dependably and meets those needs dozens of times, they come to trust that person. In response, babies offer smiles and coos and cuddles which draw the caregiver ever closer emotionally. That's parent/infant bonding. But when two unrelated adults fall in love with one another, that's attachment, too. The process of being physically attracted to a person must be followed by being emotionally drawn into a relationship that is built upon mutual trust and caring. Bonding happens between parents and children, and between brothers and sisters, but it also happens between husbands and wives, between committed life partners.

Children who have never had a one-on-one relationship with a single dependable caretaker may have a harder time attaching. Children raised by shift workers in orphanages, for example, have probably never had an attachment experience. Additionally, children who have been abused or neglected may have forged dysfunctional bonds with untrustworthy and undependable adults and so may need to learn new ways of interacting with and trusting parent figures. Such children and their parents may face some challenges to attaching, and those challenges may require special kinds of responses and support from you. The blunt truth is that love alone will not be enough for these children and families to forge tight bonds and for these children to grow up healthy. But, assuming that the family has access to good post-placement services and counseling and keeps themselves connected to the groups and books and magazines that will help them to expand that support, these children, too, will firmly attach to their new families.

📖 Learn more about it:

"Promoting Attachment through the Senses" by Patricia Irwin Johnston
  http://www.adopting.org/pat_attach.html

Launching a Baby's Adoption by Patricia Irwin Johnston (Perspectives Press, Inc., 1998)

Toddler Adoption: The Weaver's Craft by Mary Hopkins-Best (Perspectives Press, Inc., 1997)

Adopting the Hurt Child: Hope for Families with Special Needs Kids by Gregory Keck and Regina Kopecky (Pinon Press, 1995)

Attachment Disorder Network (a parent support and education organization for families parenting children with attachment problems) http://www.radzebra.org/

Parent Network for the Post Institutionalized Child http://www.pnpic.org

But They'll Be So *Different* from Us!

My friend Carol was stunned when her mother casually re-marked in front of Carol's brown-eyed toddler son that "all" of her grandchildren had blue eyes. Sherman was shocked and hurt when his parents informed him that certain "family heirlooms" would be divided among only their grandchildren by birth. Can you see yourself in either of these situations?

If you are to maintain a positive relationship with your loved ones after they become adoptive parents, you are going to have to "get over" any bias you may have toward "blood relations." Start early.

Will the fact that these kids come from a different genetic background make them "feel different"? It could. Many traits of personality are indeed genetically based. Intellectual or musical or athletic potential, a tendency toward shyness, the sense of humor, and a basic optimistic or pessimistic orientation are the kinds of traits that are pretty much "hard wired" in each indi-vidual. Additionally, there is a genetic predisposition toward some learning disabilities and some mental health problems. Atten-tion deficit disorder, for example, appears more frequently among children who have been adopted. One logical explanation for this is that people with the impulse control problems that accompany ADD are at much higher risk for experiencing an unplanned pregnancy.

But at the same time, all of our potential takes shape—or does not—within the milieu of our environment. The musical potential of a child never exposed to an instrument or to singing will likely never be revealed and enjoyed. The learning disabled child raised in a family of bookworms could experience either the pain of "not fitting" or, under more supportive circumstances, develop far beyond the potential that might have been expected had he grown up in a family that did not value or appreciate education and intellectual challenge. There can be the great joy of experiencing a previously unknown world in being the couch potato relative sitting in the stands to cheer for the breaststroker streaking down the pool.

The truth is that "claiming" children not genetically related to you may be far easier than you think. Perhaps you already have grandchildren who are more like the parent who is your in-law than like your son or daughter. Perhaps you grew up in a family where the siblings were not much alike, even though it seemed to you that your friends and their siblings had much more in common with one another in looks, likes, and tastes.

If you have not had the opportunity to observe and appreciate diametric differences in personalities and appearance between family members, you may be more challenged in this regard, but you can do it, and you *must* do so with complete devotion and complete consistency.

The alternative, quite frankly, is very clear. A parent's first obligation will always be to his children. This will be true for your family members who adopt their children. If you are unable to leap with your loved ones into adoption and are therefore unable to treat your grandchildren or nieces and nephews by birth and adoption equally, their parents may be forced to withdraw from family interactions in order to protect their children.

What about Race?

Most of us—whether we are white or black or yellow or red or brown—are more racist than we care to believe. While it's true that fewer and fewer people today are openly, hostilely racist in their outlook, beneath the surface, many may harbor racist feelings mixed into myth and stereotype. Whether the stereotyping appears positive (Asians are always smart—good at math and music. Black people have rhythm and make great athletes) or negative (Gypsies—Rom people—are thieves. Black people are lazy) it's wrong and it's damaging.

Some racism operates in "degrees." Depending on where and how and when we were raised, we may feel more or less judgmental about certain racial groups than about others. Veterans of the Pacific arena of W.W.II or the Vietnam conflict may harbor negativity about Asians. The size of the racial population in a geographic area often contributes to the level of racism there. For example racism toward Latin American people has historically been more pronounced in the Southwest than in the Midwest where Hispanic populations have, until very recently, been much smaller than in the southwest or on the coasts. The reality is, however, that there is, in most of Europe and the northern two thirds of North America, significant unacknowledged "white privilege," and whether our grandchildren are Asian or Latino or African-American, etc., they are likely to experience significant prejudice from others at some time in their lives. Additionally, the adoptive parents and any children born to them will feel this, too—as might you.

Oftentimes we feel more comfortable with people of other races than we assume people around us do. When Dave and I adopted our African-American/Latina daughter, for example, Dave's parents were supportive on the surface, but they seemed very nervous about "showing her off" to the other residents of their retirement community. We made several weeks worth of private—not secret, but private—visits to their apartment with our older two children and the new baby before they were comfortable enough to suggest that we all go down to the dining room for dinner. Their friends amazed us all with their delight over our beautiful brown baby.

You will all have much to learn as a newly multi-racial family, but, with open hearts and open minds, you can do this well—and every family come out the better for it.

📖 Learn more about it:

Two especially good websites for finding a wealth of articles on transracial adoption are those of the New York State Committee for the Concerns of Children (http://www.nysccc.org/T-Rarts/T-Rarts.html) and Pact: An Adoption Alliance (http://www.pactadopt.org)

Inside Transracial Adoption by Gail Steinberg and Beth Hall (Perspectives Press, Inc., 2000)

Dim Sum, Bagels and Grits: A Sourcebook for Multicultural Families by Myra Alperson (Farrar, Straus and Giroux, 2000)

Secret Thoughts of an Adoptive Mother by Jana Wolff (Andrews and McMeel, revised 2000)

Can Older or Disabled Children "Fit"?

Yes, most of the time healthy newborns are "easier" for families to adapt to and quicker to adapt themselves. They arrive so vulnerable that they are hard for even the steeliest-hearted to resist. They have had little opportunity to experience multiple traumas and losses. There is not much that needs to be "undone" psychologically in order to get them on the road to attachment and good mental health. But for flexible families who have been well prepared, who have had full disclosure and thus have realistic expectations about what to expect, and who have identified and are willing to turn to professional and peer support services, adopting an older child from a disadvantaged background can be an amazingly positive experience for everyone in the family.

Could this be hard on the children already in the family? Yes, it could. But follow up studies show that children raised in well prepared and supported foster families and families who adopt children with special needs become more empathic and caring and less biased than most of their peers. What a gain for everyone!

What will be most important for you to understand, should your loved ones decide to adopt older children or children with medical, mental health, or learning problems, is the importance of your offering unconditional support rather than unsolicited advice. Children with these kinds of special needs need a different approach to parenting than do children who do not have these issues. What worked or is working for you and your perfectly healthy kids from intact families will probably *not* work with these kids, so don't advise. Agencies should be preparing families carefully for these special issues and make available post-adoption support services, and most of them do. Once you know that these resources are in place for your extended family, it will be important for you to operate on the assumption that they know what they are doing. That means that they don't need you to challenge their parenting approaches, but rather to support them. They may also need emotional and physical support, because these can be trying times. If you can, offer that support, but not at the expense of subtly or directly undermining the parenting techniques that are in place in the family.

📖 Learn more about it:

A Child's Journey through Placement by Vera Fahlberg, M.D. (Perspectives Press, Inc., 1991)

Adopting the Hurt Child by Gregory Keck and Regina Kopecky (Pinon Press, 1995)

Our Own: Adopting and Parenting the Older Child by Trish Maskew (Snowcap Press, 1999)

Open Adoption? We Don't Want to Share!

In twenty years, there has been a significant change in adoption practice. Where two decades ago nearly all adoptions involved no identifying knowledge of or communication between adoptive and birth families until the child was at least of majority, now more and more adoptions involve varying degrees of openness. There are many reasons for these changes. They began, quite frankly, in response to two separate phenomena. First, adult adoptees in significant numbers were making clear that not having access to their original birth certificates and background information was creating problems for them. They began to insist on access to more information. When that information was provided, most of the time the result was positive.

Social workers took notice. Then, as single parenthood became more societally acceptable, fewer women with unintended pregnancies considered adoption. Those who did look at adoption, while feeling unprepared to parent, were not feeling as "shamed" as their sisters of previous generations and so were more assertive. They began to say to agencies something like, "Look, you wouldn't expect anyone in her right mind to hand over her child to an anonymous babysitter for even an evening, so how is it logical that you would expect me to place my child in another family for life without some information to reassure me that he will be safe and loved?"

The result was openness in adoption. It began with simple exchanges of letters facilitated by agencies or attorneys. No last names or addresses were shared. Over time, some families wished face-to-face meetings before the baby was born, again, usually without identifying information shared. The practice has evolved to include these approaches at one end of the spectrum and at-will, free access between birth and adoptive families from before birth through the child's lifetime at the other.

Has open adoption been better for kids? We don't know for sure, because there hasn't been much long-term research—yet. But proponents of open adoption believe that, theoretically, children with ready access to the information about who they look like and act like, to medical records, to reasons why adoption was chosen for them, will grow up with a greater sense of ease and confidence about themselves and both of their families than did children who grew up in an informational vacuum.

And what about the adults? Is open adoption better for them? Again, we don't know for sure, yet. Both birthparents and adoptive parents who choose openness say, anecdotally, that they know it is "right" for them. Indeed, the only really good long-term research project going on openness in families (by Ruth McRoy of University of Texas, Austin and Harold Grotevant of University of Minnesota) has made clear not that open adoption is better than confidential adoption, but that birth and adoptive parents in their study seem to feel satisfied with the particular level of openness or privacy in their adoptions when they have indeed chosen that level (as opposed to having it imposed on them). Yes, there are some complications to open adoption. Those complications are the same kinds of complications that occur with any long-term relationships. Circumstances change; people experience crises; misunderstandings happen. Maintaining a healthy open adoption requires flexibility and cooperation and support. It can work best if the professionals involved in its arrangement feel a responsibility for post adoption services too, as over the long term sometimes the assistance of an objective outside can be helpful in maintaining a long term relationship that is seen to be about what's in the best interests of the child.

📖 Learn more about it:

Adoption without Fear edited by James Gritter, M.S.W. (Corona Publishers, 1989)

Openness in Adoption: Exploring Family Connections by Harold D. Grotevant and Ruth G. McRoy (Sage Publications, 1998)

The Open Adoption Experience by Lois Ruskai Melina and Sharon Kaplan Roszia (HarperCollins, 1993)

Am I the "Real Grandparent"?

Some kids who are adopted know their birthfamilies, which may give them access to birthgrandparents. Depending on equal parts of personal dynamics and proximity, some of these grand-parents may become very involved in your grandchildren's lives. That could, at first glance, feel threatening to you. But think about this: Can a kid have too many loving aunts and uncles? No? Then why can he only have four grandparents?

The world has changed. It used to be that most kids had four grandparents—their dad's mother and father and their mom's mother and father. Times change, and now some kids have single grandparents, or they have extra sets through their membership in stepfamilies. Kids who were adopted may have extra sets too, but no longer is such a situation considered odd or unusual. Within your peer group likely most grandparents are sharing their grandparental responsibilities and rights to a beloved child with some less than traditional other folks.

Bottom line is that what makes a "real" grandparent is far less biology than it is psychology. Geography plays a significant role, too. Kids operate in a concrete, rather than an abstract world. The people who demonstrate their caring by interacting with them face-to-face, on the telephone, via computer, etc. are those who will ultimately come to feel like "real family." Ultimately, then, whether you are a grandparent by birth or by adoption, you have the power to build a success grandparental relation-ship with a child or to let it languish. You can pick up the ball and run with it, or pass it.

📖 Learn more about it:

The Open Adoption Experience by Sharon Kaplan Roszia and Lois Melina (HarperCollins, 1993)

Being a Birthparent: Finding Our Place by Brenda Romanchik (R-Squared Press, 1999)

Grandparenting with Love and Logic by Jim Fay and Foster Cline, M.D. (Love and Logic Press, 1997)

What If It Doesn't Work?

Having an adoption fall through can be absolutely devastating for everyone involved—adopters, birthparents, the child, and extended families. It's the stuff of which nightmares are made, the very worst thing that prospective adopters can imagine. These things happen infrequently, but when they happen, they may be at the birthparent's or the adoptive parents' initiative.

An incomplete adoption plan may be reversed at the birthparents' initiative. Often adopters referred to these missed opportunities as *failed adoptions, changes of heart,* or *adoption reversals.*

1. An expectant parent may decide before the baby is born or right after birth (and before placement) that she is going to parent the child after all. The adoptive parents never take custody of these children at all, though that does not seem to lessen their sense of pain and loss when the adoption they were counting on doesn't take place. Would-be adopters are being hurt by these situations far more often than ever before. Why? It is not because expectant parents are changing their minds more frequently than they were twenty years ago. In fact, it has always been the case that something close to 50% of women who seriously explore adoption eventually choose to parent. Today, however, would-be adopters are often "matched" with a pregnant woman relatively early in a pregnancy, getting to meet and know the birthparents, whereas in the days of totally confidential adoption prospective adopters were not even contacted by an agency during the birthmother's pregnancy. Instead, they waited until after the birth, after the birthmother had signed papers terminating her parental rights, before calling the adoptive family to tell them that their child—a newborn, a baby a few weeks or months old—was ready to come home.

2. The child is placed into prospective adopters' arms and they take him home and care for him for a while, only to have to return him to his birthfamily. When this happens, most of the time it is not without adopters being prepared for the possibility and being given advance warning that it is coming. Some states have what amounts to a "cooling off period," several days or a few weeks during which the mother of a newborn can place her child either with prospective adopters or into foster care while she makes a final decision. Adoptive parents in those states and provinces are well aware that the birthmother can change her mind during this period. There is also a type of placement called fost-adopt, wherein prospective adopters agree to serve as foster parents of children who have been removed from their birth homes by the state. Children who are placed with them are children that the family would be willing to adopt should their birthparents not succeed in "getting their acts together" in hopes of reclaiming their children after several months.

3. Very rarely indeed a birthparent may demand a child back long after the law appears to give them a right to do so. These are the Baby Jessica and Baby Richard and Baby Jesse cases that capture so much media attention. They can happen only when the law has not been properly followed. A birthfather's rights have not been appropriately terminated, for example, or a birthmother can prove that she was coerced. These things almost never happen to families who use careful, reputable, ethical service providers.

Adoptions also may end at the adopting parent's initiative.

1. An adoptive family receives a referral on a child from another country and travels to bring that child home, only to find once there that the child's problems are far more serious than they believed them to be. They refuse the

placement. Most often these parents are quickly matched with another child and do come home to the U.S. as parents.

2. Adoptive parents receive a child—usually an older child, either domestically or internationally—fully intending to adopt and raise that child. Sometime after the placement it becomes clear that the family is unable to parent this child. This may happen for a variety of possible reasons, but nearly always it involves a combination of the family being inaccurately or incompletely informed of the child's special needs and their being inappropriately prepared, so that they have unrealistic expectations. When this happens before an adoption is finalized, so that the child returns to the custody of the placing agency, it is called a *disruption*. When (much rarer) it happens after an adoption has already been finalized, so that the family must seek the help of an agency to take custody of the child and relinquish their legal parental rights, it is called a *dissolution*.

No matter how the undoing of a hoped for adoption occurs, the loss is huge for the family. When they have experienced a failed adoption initiated by birthparents, their grief may include either their feeling betrayed (by the professional, by the birthfamily) or their blaming themselves (for not paying close enough attention to "signs" or for not being "good enough to convince her"). When the adopters themselves initiate the disruption or dissolution, it is often accompanied by guilt and shame at not being able to "tough it out" and be "good enough parents." In either case these parents carry great pain and loss and regret and often worry a great deal about the well-being of the child they are no longer parenting.

This is a loss with similarities to pregnancy loss and neonatal death, yet it is different. Having it happen "early" does not necessarily "make it easier." Whatever you do, don't suggest that this has happened "for the best." Don't offer platitudes at all. Instead, just be there to help absorb some of the shock and grief and loss and allow this family to grieve at their own pace.

📖 Learn more about it:

"Losing an Adoption" Practical Advice for Moving On after a Uniquely Painful Experience" by Wendy Williams and Patricia Irwin Johnston
http://www.perspectivespress.com/losingadopt.html

"Losing a Sibling: Helping Your Child Cope with Adoption Reversal" by Wendy Williams and Patricia Irwin Johnston
http://www.perspectivespress.com/siblingloss.html

Turning Loss into Gain

Adoption is not a choice that anyone makes lightly. In fact, doing so would be next to impossible. The process of adoption is complex, involving many decisions, lots of paperwork, screening, and preparation. For most, it feels invasive of cherished privacy. It can be expensive, and, unlike giving birth, few (if any) of its costs are covered by insurance.

In order to have come to the decision to adopt, your family member has very likely spent months—even years—sorting through options in order to make a decision. So why has adoption come as a "surprise" to you?

Let's face facts. Few adult children announce to their family at Sunday dinner, "Mom, Dad, we've decided to get pregnant! Sandy and I are throwing away the birth control and we will be having sex every Tuesday and Thursday and Saturday for as long as it takes to get pregnant. Any advice you have on that?"

Few adults engage their sisters and brothers in a conversation something like, "Harry, Rebecca, your kids are really so attractive, and you seem to have had them so easily. Tell me, what positions for intercourse did you use to conceive those great little guys and how often did you have to do it?"

Few adults ask, "Tell me, family, what do you think. I'm 35 and single and I want a kid, so I'm trying to decide whether to have unprotected sex with this guy I've been dating casually and hope to get pregnant, or do donor insemination, or adopt. Care to give me your opinion?"

The fact is that family planning is a highly personal issue. While some folks don't seem to do much planning—they just conceive by accident and deal with the consequences—for most members of the post birth-control generations family planning is taken pretty seriously. It's true that some take this ability for granted, not thinking that the ability to postpone or avoid pregnancy today might find them unable to become pregnant later, but even that is not the issue here. The issue is that your family members will be making their own decisions about whether, when, and how to add a child to their family. Hey, did you share personal issues like this and seek approval for your family planning decisions with *your* parents, with *your* brothers and sisters, with *your* good friends?

📖 Learn more about it:

Parents at Last: Celebrating Adoption and the New Pathways to Parenthood by Cynthia V.N. Peck and Wendy Wilkinson (Clarkson Potter, 1998)

Understanding Infertility: Insights for Family and Friends by Patricia Irwin Johnston (Perspectives Press, Inc., 1996).

Adopting on Your Own: The Compete Guide to Adopting as a Single Parent by Lee Varon (Farrar, Straus and Giroux, 2000)

Lesbian and Gay Fostering and Adoption by Stephen Hicks and Janet McDermott (1999)

A Passage to the Heart edited by Amy Klatzkin (Yeong & Yeong Book Co., 1999)

Our Own: Adopting and Parenting the Older Child by Trish Maskew (Snowcap Press, 1999)

Why Am I Hesitating?

If your loved ones have not kept you in the loop about the fact that they were thinking about starting or adding to their family through adoption, their announcement may have been quite a shock. In that case, I'm going to give you the break that these folks—who are very likely feeling defensive and frightened and disappointed about your reaction—may be unable to give you. That break is acknowledging that your hesitancy about adoption is normal and forgivable—even though it isn't OK.

Those of us who live adoption wish it were not so, but at first glance adoption seems "second best" to most people. We have begun to call this bias *adoptism*, and we will talk about addressing this bias in the world at large in the last section of this book. Without being given the opportunity to learn more about adoption, you may be feeling this "second best" fear and wanting "more" for yourself and your children. After all, most of us (including your children) come to adulthood with certain expectations about the definition of family. We may have thought of "family" as consisting of a mother, a father, and a child to whom they have given birth. But the reality is that in 21st Century North America the definition of family has expanded to embrace one parent "families," same-sex-couple parented "families," childfree "families," yours-mine-and-ours "families," and more. Some of your peers may be serving as primary parents for their grandchildren.

Okay, so you may be able to acknowledge these broad philosophical realities, but on a personal level, this still seems to hurt. You may not even be sure why it hurts. I think I know.

For everyone it touches—birthparents, adopted people, adoptive parents, extended birth and adoptive families—adoption is a blend of gain and loss. Those losses are the root of the pain. Whether your children were infertile, single, or gay/lesbian as they worked through their frustrated desires to become parents, some losses that eventually led them to consider and then embrace adoption included these...

- The loss of the common expectation that one will blend his or her genes with those of a much loved partner to create a unique human being who is the ultimate expression of the love they share.

- The loss of the opportunity to make someone pregnant or to become pregnant and to experience the physical and emotional benefits and expectations our culture has taught us to desire and expect from pregnancy and birth.

- The loss of not just their individual genetic continuity, but, yours, too—their expectation that they would be extending the family blood line—your blood line—into the future.

- The potential loss of the opportunity to parent at all.

If your family members were "preferential adopters" like Ruben and Anita, who have already given birth to children and could do so again, but instead are adopting by choice, the above losses may not be part of their decision to adopt (though, even for preferential adopters this lack of genetic connection will be a real loss eventually for them and for their adopted child and perhaps for you). But preferential adopters join all other adopters in another of adoption's central losses:

- The loss of control over privacy in family planning that those who do not adopt take completely for granted.

These adults have spent months, perhaps years, coming to the decision to adopt. They have worked through their own questions and fears and much of their pain, and they are working hard to keep the rest of it under control in order to accomplish an important mission: to bring their child home.

A truth about dealing with loss is that sometimes those who are immersed in the pain of loss lose sight of the fact that others can be hurting, too. Just as your children have experienced loss before coming to the decision to gain a child through adoption, you, too are experiencing loss, and they may not have realized this. In fact, you may not have realized this yourself until now. You, too, are experiencing a number of lost expectations:

- You expected your grandchildren to be born to their parents—your children.

- You expected them to be genetically related to you and so to be similar to you in looks, in personality, in race.

- You expected them to arrive after a nine-month pregnancy that the whole family would experience vicariously.

- You expected them to come as newborns.

- You expected that they would "belong" to just your family (well, maybe you'd be sharing them with those in-laws, too).

- You certainly did not expect that your children—and, by extension, you and the rest of your family—would have to be subjected to an "approval" process before receiving a child.

- And, finally, if your children are part of a non-traditional family (single parents, gay/lesbian couples, older couples, remarried step families) you may already have done the very private work of grieving for the losses related to those "differences," assumed that there would be no grandchildren from them, and may now be frightened about having to deal with the very real and very vocal disapproval of other family and friends that such folks would deign to become parents at all!

📖 Learn more about it:

Adopting after Infertility by Patricia Irwin Johnston (Perspectives Press, Inc., 1992)

Being Out of Control of "Making It Better"

As parents, you and I know something that your kids may not yet know—parenting is a lifetime function. Even after our kids are grown, we parents have a really hard time seeing our children in pain, and despite our best efforts, sometimes we just can't help but try to fix the booboos, even for our adult children. But let's get real: you can't make your gay child straight; you can't make your infertile child fertile; you can't get your single child a partner; you can't make a bad marriage good and prevent the divorce.

> Rachael told me, "One issue that we've found hard is that my husband's parents disagree with us about how far to go in infertility treatment before adoption. We never did IVF and decided very quickly that adoption was for us. We are very happy with our decision. However my husband's parents have problems accepting the adoption plans because they feel we should have gone further down the treatment path. They have definitely grown up with the idea that adoption is second best and have been brainwashed by the 'marvels of medicine' outlook."

I can explain to your adult child, after the fact, that you meant well when you offered all of that unsolicited advice about what to do *instead of* adopting. But explaining won't change the fact that these folks in crisis, who have made a hard decision, may just have heard from you what appears to be a giant put-down of their carefully-made choice. They have come to see adoption as a *positive choice*—second choice, perhaps, but far from second best!

Let me say this again, because it is key to "getting it" when it comes to understanding and embracing your son or daughter's decision to adopt. Adoption may not even have appeared on the menu when this son or daughter first begin to explore parenting, so adoption may have come as a second choice. *But* those who do eventually choose to adopt have most often read and read, attended meetings and conferences, solicited the advice of experts, and talked thoroughly into many long nights with their partners. By the time they announce to you that you are expecting a grandchild by adoption, they have become excited, and their own thinking about adoption has become so highly evolved that they may be deeply offended by the thought that anyone would see adoption as second best. That that "second best" thinking comes from their parents is especially hurtful.

What to Say and What Not

Rather than blurt out, "Oh no! Why would you do that?" or "Must you? Have you tried everything?" it would be absolutely wonderful if you could have the presence of mind to pause, reflect, and then say instead, "Wow! That comes as a surprise. Dad and I didn't have any idea you were thinking about adopting. We don't know much about adoption, so you can imagine that we're going to need some time to get up to speed on this. Will you help us?"

But probably 95 out of 100 prospective adoptive grandparents or about-to-be aunts and uncles don't think this quickly, so you are not alone. No, you probably reacted just like the families of Melika and Ahmad, Nancy and Fred, Sam and Stewart, Marcia and Erv, Ruben and Anita, and Margaret. In your shock and surprise, you probably simply blurted out the first thing that came into your head, and because you didn't know much about adoption, that surprise was mixed with myth and with fear, which came pouring out, too.

So You've Already Blown It

If you have already reacted like the families of Melika and Ahmad, Nancy and Fred, Sam and Stewart, Marcia and Erv, Ruben and Anita, and Margaret, your children were probably hurt and angry about your response. You've had many years of experience with your loved ones' reactions to pain and anger. Do they explode? Do they hold it inside? Do they go away mad? Do they regroup and come back to discuss it or to argue? It's very important to your family's future that you not allow this unsettling event to go undiscussed and unresolved. This breach can be mended.

First, you have some learning to do. The rest of this book will give you the opportunity to understand why you initially reacted as you did, will give you some accurate facts about adoption, and will help you to face your children's losses, your prospective grandchildren's losses and your own losses. All of this acknowledgement of *losses* will help you to embrace the *gains* for all of you that come with adoption. Though *Adoption Is a Family Affair!* is not designed to provide exhaustive coverage of these subjects, it will cover the most important points you need to know and then guide those who want or need more information to more detailed coverage elsewhere.

How Adoption Works:
The Facts vs. the Myths

I moderate several Internet discussion boards for those who are exploring adoption, waiting to adopt, or parenting in adoption. Family reaction to their adoption plans is a frequent topic of discussion on these boards.

> Paul reported, "Although she is surprisingly excited for us, my mother-in-law seems to have the attitude that we will be in some sort of custodial relationship with the adopted child. It's as if she thinks that, at the end of it all (like maybe when the child is an adult), the birthmother would then resume parental status. (That's probably not exactly how she sees it, but it's something weird like that). She seems to think that's appropriate."

> Leslie offered, "I am still having trouble with my mother-in-law telling me that it is good that I am thinking of adopting because I will probably get pregnant now that I will be able to relax. Regardless of how many times I have explained it in the past several years and no matter how many

things I have given her to read regarding this stupid statement, she still prefers to believe these myths that she hears from her friends. It is really making me feel very negatively towards my mother-in-law."

Bonnie added, "Even after seeing his referral picture and hearing how healthy he is described to be, my sister-in-law is absolutely convinced that our foreign-born son will have been abused and neglected beyond help or hope in some institution in his birth country. It's as if she's expecting him to grow up to be an ax murderer or something!"

"Just Relax: After Adopting, You'll Get Pregnant"

Let's toss this old saw off the pile first off, because it is perhaps the single most offensive (not to mention most common) myth-ridden comment I've heard during thirty years of being infertile myself and working with infertile couples. We hear this over and over and over.

During the past quarter of a century a number of studies have been done which show unequivocally that relaxing alone after adopting does not produce pregnancies. Adoption did not result in conception thirty years ago, it didn't fifteen years ago, and it doesn't this year.

Though everyone knows someone whose third cousin or next door neighbor conceived right away after adopting, statistically the facts are these: Five percent of infertile couples will spontaneously conceive after ending fertility treatment and then adopting. This is exactly the same percentage of folks who will conceive following the end of fertility treatment without adopting.

What folks fail to consider when they make the assumption that a pregnancy after adopting was due to "relaxing" is that the expectant couple may not have ended treatment. Though most adoption professionals and counseling professionals working with infertile people feel strongly that one should not pursue adoption and infertility treatment at the same time, many somewhat desperate couples do so anyway. They hide this fact from the adoption professionals with whom they are working, as well as from their families and friends.

The reason that the "Oh, good, now you'll get pregnant" comments are so offensive to infertile couples is similar to the reasons why comments like, "Oh, you're adopting? I'm so sorry," or "Do you have any children of your own?" are offensive—adoptism! These comments carry with them the implication that, in the speaker's opinion, at least, adopting a child is not "good enough," is not "real parenting," is "second best and second rate family building."

When prospective adopters hear this thinking from the people closest to them, they wonder how their children will be treated within the family circle. This is a real and logical concern. Indeed, if you feel this way, if you harbor this hope for a genetic grandchild after the adopted one, will you be able to treat these children as equal members of the family?

Statistics

In addition to about 50,000 situations where stepparents adopt their partner's children or grandparents or other kin adopt a relative's child, in the United States there are about 50,000 non-relative adoptions each year. Because the government has not provided funding for legislation passed years ago to require that states keep and report accurate adoption statistics, the precise breakdown of how many children are adopted domestically each year, what proportion of them are infants or toddlers or older children, how many are adopted through public agencies or private agencies or independent of agencies, etc. is not available. The only accurate and reliable statistics about adoptions by U.S. citizens are those kept by the Immigration and Naturalization Service (INS) related to international adoptions. Those statistics are reported annually in January for the governmental fiscal year ending the prior September 30th. The statistics reported in 2000, for example, show that there were 16,396 international adoptions in FY1999, up 4% from the prior year. The top twenty sending countries during 1999 were Russia (4348 children), mainland China (4101), South Korean (2008), Guatemala (1002), Romania (895), Vietnam (709), India (499), Ukraine (323), Cambodia (249), Colombia (231), Bulgaria (221), Philippines (195), Mexico (137), Kazakhstan (113), Ethiopia (103), Poland (97), Haiti (96), Thailand (77), Brazil (64), Lithuania (63), Moldavia (63), with the remaining 802 children adopted internationally coming from a variety of other countries.

The Kids

It is simply not true that there are no babies to adopt. Thousands of healthy children under a year of age are adopted domestically and internationally each year. A small number of U.S.-born babies are even adopted by residents of other countries. A high proportion of infant adoptions are done through private agencies—often, but not always, these are religiously sponsored not-for-profits—or are done through a direct connection between adoptive parents and birthparents in an arrangement called a "private" or "independent" adoption.

In addition, thousands more U.S.-born children identified as having special needs are adopted each year. Most of these adoptions are handled by the public agencies in each state which are variously called the Department of Family and Children's Services, the Public Welfare Department, etc. In some areas, the state has contracted with one or more private child welfare agencies to handle recruitment, preparation, placement, and supervision of families adopting children with special needs.

Children are classified as having "special needs" for a variety of reasons. Sometimes it's only because of their age. A child who becomes available as a school-aged child is considered more difficult to place than are infants or toddlers no matter what the state of his health.

Some children's label of "special needs" is given because they come with two or more siblings. Three brothers and sisters may be healthy emotionally and physically and continue to wait because it is harder to recruit parents for a ready-made multi-child family.

Some older waiting children have medical problems (some chronic, some correctable), or learning differences, or emotional problems. Some, but far from all, have serious ongoing problems related to having been abused or neglected in prior settings.

Some children—including babies—wait for families and are considered to have special needs because they are children of color. A higher proportion of adults of color adopt than do whites, but there are still not enough people of color to adopt the children of color waiting for permanent families. More children of color are part of the system because proportionately higher numbers of parents of color live in poverty, which creates or contributes to many of the difficulties which bring their children into the foster care and adoption systems.

No matter what his age or condition, and no matter what the financial status of the adults who want to adopt him, once a child has been designated by his agency to have "special needs" he is eligible for special financial support from state and federal governments. This support, called a *subsidy* or *adoption assistance*, which may also include Medicaid benefits, is available until he is 18 to help his adopting parents obtain the medical or educational or counseling assistance necessary to meet his particular special needs.

The single most important statistic for you to hear, hold close, and understand about adoption is that, despite the myths out there and the horror stories reported in the media, repeated studies show that the overwhelming majority of children who join their families by adoption fare well, forge close bonds with their families, and grow up to be every bit as well adjusted as their non-adopted peers.

That's a fact, not a wish.

📖 Learn more about it:

Growing Up Adopted: A Portrait of Adolescents and Their Parents by Peter L. Benson, Ph.D, Anu Sharma Ph.D. and Eugene C. Roehlkepartain (Minneapolis: The Search Institute, 1994)

How People Adopt

Adoption can be arranged in three ways:

- Through public agencies sponsored by individual state governments, usually with county offices. Children with special needs most often are placed through public agencies or through them with the help of subcontracting private agencies. A relatively small number of healthy newborn infants—in particular Caucasian infants—are placed through public agencies.

- Through private not-for-profit, state-licensed agencies, which often, but not always, have a religious affiliation. Most agency adoptions of domestically-born infants and most international adoptions are handled in this way.

- Privately or independently. Technically, this is defined as an adoption directly arranged between birthfamilies and adoptive families, and historically connections were made by a family physician, clergyperson or friend of the family. Today such connections are the exception rather than the rule. Most private adoptions are arranged with the assistance of a businessperson—most often either an attorney or an unlicensed consultant called a facilitator—who advises would-be parents on how to market themselves to expectant parents considering planning an adoption.

Would-be adopters choose their route to adoption based on a number of factors. Some prospective parents have problems meeting the screening requirements of some (but not all) private agencies because of their age or their religion or their sexual orientation or their marital status or the length of their marriage or a history of divorce. This then leads them to look at public agency adoption or independent adoption. Some feel more comfortable knowing that a licensed agency staffed by professionals with social work experience is screening and counseling birthparents and matching them, while others want the control they think they gain by doing their own advertising and screening and match making, independent of an agency. Some have strong feelings either for or against open adoption and make their choice of intermediary based upon a matching philosophy. Many adopters want to work only with agents within their own state. A contributing factor in the selection of a style and a route to adoption is often cost.

Those who feel prepared only to adopt a newborn will probably find the waiting times at public agencies to be a barrier and so will explore private agency or independent adoption. On the other hand, those who are seeking to adopt older children or a sibling group will find their needs met most quickly and effectively through the public agency. When one has fallen in love with the idea of adopting a non-U.S.-born child from a particular country, one chooses an agency experienced in working with that country's governmental regulations.

For most of those reading this book, the adult family members who are adopting have already made their choices about who to adopt and how to adopt and where to adopt. They will fill you in on the details, but that doesn't open the door for you to try to change their minds. You must trust that they have made these choices carefully, after reading, attending meetings, using face-to-face and Internet support groups, etc. You can use these same resources to learn more.

📖 Learn more about it:

Adoption: The Tapestry Guide by Laurie Wallmark (Tapestry Books, 1998)

The Adoption Resource Book by Lois Gilman (HarperCollins, revised 1998)

Adopting and Advocating for the Special Needs Child by Rita Laws and L Anne Babb (Greenwood, 1999)

How to Adopt Internationally: A Guide for Agency-Directed and Independent Adoption (2000-20002 Edition) by Jean Nelson-Erichsen and Heino R. Erichsen (Mesa House Publishing, 2000)

The Cost

One does not have to be wealthy to adopt. Instead, prospective adopters are expected to demonstrate that they can effectively manage the money they actually have and can provide a safe and healthy environment in which to raise a child.

The costs involved in completing an adoption can vary significantly—from the $6 cost of a workbook used in a preparation class to $50,000 in some cases. All adoptions, however, have certain requirements regardless of who is picking up the fees for service. These include:

- a homestudy or parent preparation and counseling
- document preparation
- legal fees
- travel costs (state-to-state or internationally) in many cases

Families willing to adopt a US-born child identified as having special needs will find that fees are low to non-existent at public agencies, and that their children's needs often make them eligible for some ongoing financial assistance or medical care or mental health counseling. Subsidies are not based on the income of the would-be adopters, but instead on the needs of the child eligible for adoption. Working through this "system" can be complicated, but is worthwhile. Information and support is often best found through local adoptive family support groups.

International adoptions are usually more expensive than are domestic adoptions. Most agencies placing children from other countries receive no support from the state or federal government, so adopters must absorb the costs. Most often they will pay a flat administrative program fee to the local agency that handles their adoption, administrative and legal costs to the overseas agent or agency, and often a "donation" to the orphanage that cared for their child. Travel costs are higher, too. Whether would-be adopters choose to travel abroad to bring their child home or use the services of an escort to bring their child home to them, the cost of international travel (in time, and, sometimes in lost salary, too) is a significant consideration in planning an adoption. More and more adopters are embracing the idea of traveling to meet their child in his country of origin. This gives them an opportunity to observe and learn about the culture they will one day help their child to explore, to see and ask questions about his present environment so that they can provider a smoother transition, and to take many pictures and gather mementos that they can later share with their child.

On top of these expenses, infertile couples have probably spent considerable money on unsuccessful treatment—much of it not covered by health insurance. They may have maxed out credit cards, or borrowed against home equity or life insurance. Though about 30% of employers today offer some financial support for adopters, rarely does this perk pay as high a percentage of the cost of adoption as health insurance pays for the birth of a child. Depending on income, a limited amount of adoption experiences can be taken as a tax credit.

Finances, then, are one place where family and close friends who are able to do so could demonstrate their unqualified support of adoption and make a genuine difference in their loved ones' lives. Can you "float a loan?" Might you offer a planned "inheritance" a little early? Could the extended family have a "money shower" rather than a traditional clothing and equipment shower? If you can, please offer. A timely financial gift or a loan can smooth the way and will speak volumes about your support for this route to expanding the family.

📖 Learn more about it:

"The Financial Impact of Parenthood" by Patricia Irwin
Johnston
http://www.perspectivespress.com/adoptionfinances.html

"Guide to Adoption Benefits" from the Dave Thomas
Foundation for Adoption
http://www.davethomasfoundationforadoption.org/
resource/4_3benef/index.html

"How to Make Adoption an Affordable Option" from the
National Endowment for Financial Education is available on the Internet at http://www.nefe.org

*Adoption and Financial Assistance: Tools for Navigating the
Bureaucracy* by Rita Laws and Tim O'Hanlon (Bergin &
Garvey, 1999

Changing Practice—Open Adoption vs. Confidential Adoption

Open adoption is communication and cooperation between
two families—birth and adoptive—that benefits a child loved
and cared about by everyone. Open adoption is *not* temporary
custody. Open adoption does *not* enhance the risk of a change
of heart or lead to "taking the child back." Open adoption is *not*
co-parenting. Adopted children have one set of legal, social, and
decision-making parents—their adopters. It is unusual for open
adoptions to create unmanageable problems between families.

Adoption itself is a relatively new legal institution. Though
societies across the world have always created ways to care for
children in need of replacement parents, in the U.S. adoption of
the children of "strangers" was not part of the legal system until

the very late nineteenth and early twentieth centuries. In fact, it was not until the 1930s that all U.S. states had adoption laws on their books. When adoption was informal, it was almost always arranged between kin or between families who knew one another. Not until it became formalized, occurring with the state and/or child welfare agencies serving as the intermediaries between families who were unknown to one another did adoption become "closed" and original birth records become sealed. In those times, the reasons given for supporting confidentiality were not about fears that birth and adoptive families would bring one another harm, but were instead centered on protecting the parties to the adoption from issues of shame—shame about out-of-wedlock pregnancy, shame about infertility, shame about illegitimacy.

Now, practice is changing again. In response both to changing societal mores and to birthparents and adult adoptees who have made clear that the secrecy encouraged more by society than adoption professionals for many years had not served them well, adoption is becoming more open. The degree of openness occurs on a very broad continuum. People who have already grown to adulthood in adoption—as well as their birth and adoptive parents and the professionals who arranged their adoptions—are, in large numbers, coming to believe that the total secrecy of old style confidential adoption (and, at the very least, the inability of adopted adults to have access to their original birth certificates and genetic and social information about their origins) did them all more harm than good.

Few adoptions today are completely open—which would mean that there is ongoing contact and visiting and phone calls at will between members of the birth and adoptive families. However, more and more adoptions involve some degree of openness. In some cases detailed, but non-identifying information is shared by adopting parents on profiles read by birthparents who are given the option of selecting the parents who will adopt their babies. In others, expectant parents and would-be adopters meet occasionally, but only during the pregnancy. In still others, agreements are made to share letters back and forth for some period of time (or forever) using the adoption agent as the intermediary. Letters may be sent directly to one another without plans for face-to-face visits, while other sets of parents schedule periodic visits, or even at-will, unrestricted access to one another, much as extended families interact.

Over time, adoptions with some degree of openness tend to become more, rather than less, open, as birth and adoptive families settle into their roles and become comfortable with one another and their mutual good intentions on behalf of the children both families love. However, just as do all human relationships, those in open adoptions evolve and change over time, most often in response to changes in circumstances within the families. For example, it is not uncommon for birthparents who are highly involved at first to become less involved as their grief abates. Nor is it unusual for birthparents who subsequently marry and begin to parent children to find themselves so caught up in the busyness of their family life that they take less time communicating with the family of the child for whom they chose an adoption. On the other hand, it's important for adopting families to realize that sometimes the changes in birthparents' communication has to do with their grief and pain or even shame. Families in open adoptions need to do their best to be attuned to one another and to remain adaptable over time.

While more and more infant adoptions involve some degree of openness, in the U.S. some birthparents continue to feel that they do not want ongoing communication with the children for whom they plan an adoption. There continue to be traditional agencies who support this interest in confidentiality. Additionally, the agencies responsible for finding permanency for some children who come from abusive and neglectful backgrounds find in many, but not all, situations that ongoing contact with birth families is not in a child's best interests.

Mostly because of the cultural imperatives of the countries of origin, most international adoptions today begin as closed or confidential, with little, if any information about birth families, let alone contact with them. There are exceptions to this, however, especially in adoptions from Eastern European countries, and even Asian adoptions are becoming communicative to the extent that growing numbers of adult adoptees are being helped to make contact with their families of origin. Where once adoptive parents could be certain that, whether their children needed or wanted contact with birthfamily or not, it would not be possible in international adoption, this, too, is changing rapidly.

The real directional change in adoption is not about openness versus confidentiality. It is about seeing each adoption as a unique arrangement between unique birth and adoptive families. The trend is away from "cookie cutter" practices and toward making the best decisions and supporting the best arrangements for a particular child and his two families, birth and adoptive.

📖 Learn more about it:

The Spirit of Open Adoption by James Gritter (Child Welfare League of America, 1998)

The Homestudy/Family Preparation

What used to be called a homestudy is now often called parent preparation. The change in terminology reflects a change in what the process is all about. Adoption is an institution designed primarily to meet the needs of children. Subsequently, the purpose of the homestudy/parent preparation process has become less about weeding folks in or out of the process and more about preparing them for the tasks unique to parenting children to whom they are not genetically related.

Most homestudies are completed before the arrival of a child. In a few states, the law allows for a waiver of the pre-placement homestudy for those who will be adopting independently of an agency. In those cases, what is required instead are that a report and evaluation—sometimes, but not always, less stringent and detailed than a pre-placement homestudy—be provided to the court within weeks after the placement and most certainly before the adoption can be finalized.

Being completely truthful in completing questionnaires and answering interview questions is imperative. It is always in a family's best interests to be "up front" with the social workers who will conduct their homestudy about any issues they fear will become red flags. Indeed, being discovered in a deception is worse and could, in fact, lead an agency to reject an applicant.

For international adoptions a police background check is required. Many states now require that same step for domestic adopting parents. Since juvenile records are usually sealed, this check takes into account the would-be parent's adult behaviors. Past problems with the law are evaluated carefully. Youthful indiscretions which are not part of a continuing pattern of serious problems (such as drunk driving, for example) are usually not cause for rejection.

During the preparation process parents will be asked to provide a health evaluation. The purpose, after all, is to provide permanency for children, so parents with life-shortening medical conditions often find it difficult to adopt. Would-be adopters who have chronic health problems or physical disabilities which are not life-shortening are asked to provide evidence that they have in place a plan which acknowledges and addresses any difficulties in caring for their children and keeping them safe. Similarly, single adopters are usually required to demonstrate that they have in place a guardianship plan for their children should something happen to them. Mental health will also be examined. Some agencies require that applicants take a psychological screening test such as the Minnesota Multiphasic Personality Inventory. All will ask about whether either parent has been treated in the past by a mental health professional. Adopters often fear that disclosure of treatment for depression will exclude them from the adoption process. Since depression is a common problem, it is rarely a "stopper." Indeed, most social workers are enlightened enough to recognize that those who acknowledge and seek treatment for their own problems are more likely to be willing and able to look for problems their children may have and seek out help promptly. Applicants with chronic mental health problems, such as bipolar disorder, will come under closer scrutiny. They will be asked to demonstrate, with the support and verification of their physician, that they have been and will continue to be conscientious about using the medications that keep the condition under control.

Adopters are not required to be homeowners. Evaluation of the living environment takes into account that the home is clean and safe. When the family is considering adopting a child with a disability, they are expected to share their plans for making the home accessible to the new family member.

Applicants are required to provide references. While some of these may come from family members, such as you, most will come from friends, from a neighbor, from employers, perhaps from clergy. Most agencies provide a model or outline explaining what kind of information they expect references to provide on behalf of the applicant. When that information is not provided, it is appropriate to ask for guidance with this.

If the adopters are a couple, part of the process will be to evaluate the stability of the relationship of the parenting partners. Each will be interviewed separately and there will be joint interviews as well. Most often each will be asked to write an autobiographical essay which will be used as a basis for some of that interviewing. The worker will ask about one's own family background and current state of extended family relationships. Sometimes adopters worry that their choice to distance themselves from family relationships they consider to be toxic will work against them. Usually this is not the case. In fact, social workers look favorably on singles and couples who have developed their own "extended family" relationships among close friends.

Parenting style, ethics and morality, and religious practice will be discussed in the interview process. Practicing a religion is not a legal requirement for adoption, but it may be an agency-based requirement when adopting from a religiously affiliated organization. Prior marriages must be disclosed and will be discussed. Agencies will want check to be certain that absent parents are behaving responsibly concerning child support payments.

Most of the time, but unfortunately not always, prospective adopters will spend some sessions with other would-be adopters learning about adoption's life long ramifications for all whom it touches. They may be asked to read books, to do "homework" exercises. They may listen to presentations by birthparents, adult adoptees, and experienced adoptive parents. Most especially those who are adopting children with special needs will undergo many sessions of training to help them deal with their coming child's unique issues. Some would-be adopters undergo the same training as would foster care providers.

All adults living in the home where the child will be raised are expected to be part of the preparation and evaluation process. Unless they live with the would-be parents, extended family members are rarely part of this evaluation process. If the family is already parenting children, however, those children are interviewed as well, and, depending on their age, they may be offered the opportunity to learn more about adoption themselves.

Prospective adopters often dread the concept of the parent preparation process. This is partly because they resent having to "prove themselves worthy" when those who give birth to children do not have to be "licensed to parent." The are also fearful of the unknown and the unexpected. Most adopters will later admit, however, that they are grateful for what they learned during the parent preparation process, and actually wish that they had paid more careful attention!

Getting Ready

The time between getting all of the paperwork completed and being approved by the agency (akin to having a pregnancy confirmed) and the arrival of a child is awkward for many expectant adopters. Though they now are officially expecting to become parents, they have no guaranteed timeline on which to operate. What's more, because their bellies don't expand, their "pregnancy" is an invisible one. They may be feeling that they are "part of the club" of expectant parents, but the world at large often doesn't seem them as such.

Supportive friends and family often report feeling that they are in some kind of emotional limbo with their loved ones who are expecting to adopt. If they check in "too often" for an update, they may be faced with an irritated, on-edge mommy-to-be who doesn't have any news and feels harassed by questions. If they don't ask at all, they fear that they'll be accused of not caring. Frankly, this limbo period is a real problem. The best way to address it is directly. "Son," you might say, "we're eager to know everything you're willing or able to tell us about when our grandchild will arrive. We understand, though, that a lot about this process is unpredictable, and we don't want to upset you by asking too often. We'd like you to take the lead here. How can we best get the updates we'd like to have without burdening you?

What can we do to support both your wait and your process for getting ready."

The Wait

Here's how it will go... Once adopters have completed the homestudy/preparation process, the wait for their child's referral and then arrival begins. What happens during the waiting time varies substantially depending on the style of the adoption.

International

For example, those who are adopting internationally will spend substantial time apart from the homestudy filling out and submitting documents required by the Immigration and Naturalization Service and the chosen sending country. This can be time-consuming and frustrating. Once this is accomplished they will wait for their agency to send them a "referral"—a picture of a child they could adopt, accompanied by a profile. The may receive more than one referral before they decide to say yes, and it is important that they carefully evaluate the material in the profile. More and more international adopters are using the services of special international adoption medical clinics. There, teams of physicians, therapists, mental health professionals, etc. can evaluate the profiled material. In many cases they can also view a videotape provided by the agency or orphanage in the sending country. They then use all of these tools to make recommendations to the family about the child's prognosis, or, at the very least, to suggest more questions that need to be asked.

Referrals for international adoptions are most often "sure things." These are often children who have been legally abandoned in their countries of origin. Often their birthparents are unknown, and when they are known, their rights have almost always been officially terminated already. Things can go wrong, of course. For example, children may become ill and die. But most of the time once a referral has been accepted, the next part of the waiting period is filled with the happy anticipation of getting house and home and heart ready for parenting… not to mention preparing to travel!

Special Needs Placements

Families pursuing adoption of a child with special needs may spend lots of time pouring over photolisting books from their own and other states or visiting many Internet sites that feature the profiles and photographs of waiting children. When their interest in a particular child is piqued, they will then either contact their own social worker for more information or make a contact on their own with the child's worker, who, if interested may invite them to submit their homestudy and profile for consideration.

Domestic Infant Placement

Those adopting infants domestically may or may not spend the next weeks and months actively marketing themselves. Those adopting independently (with an attorney or a facilitator) will almost surely go through these steps. Many of those adopting through agencies will too, though with most licensed agencies all there is to this step is developing an attractive and careful profile called a portfolio to be shared with expectant parents asking for the opportunity to select their child's adopting parents.

The "marketing" process can be emotionally arduous. Couples may send letters with their profiles enclosed to lists of friends and family or call their friends who are already parents and ask for their help in spreading the word that they are eager to adopt. Some family members and friends feel awkward and unwilling to be a part of this process, and that needs to be accepted as perfectly OK.

The adopters may advertise in newspapers at home or in other cities, in campus papers, on bulletin boards, on Internet sites. They may install a separate telephone line (the "baby phone") to receive calls coming from these ads. When they do, they may receive no calls at all, which can be very disheartening, or they may receive many calls at all hours of the day and night. Some will be legitimate tentative inquiries from pregnant women. Others will be from cranks. Occasionally the family will be contacted by people whose sole interest is in trying to con vulnerable people. Imagine yourself in this position—your heart skipping a beat every time the phone rings!

Eventually they will be "matched" with a woman (or a couple) dealing with an untimely pregnancy who selects them as the "right family" for her baby. These selections may be made after birthparents view the would-be adopters' profile from among those on file at an agency, or after speaking with them several times by telephone or meeting them face-to-face. This is a thrilling moment for adopters and their families!

Cautious optimism, however, is called for. Even a woman who, throughout her pregnancy, feels absolutely certain that adoption is the right choice for her (including those who have had the very best of preparation by professional counselors) must make the adoption decision all over again once the baby is born and becomes a "real person" laid in her arms. A change of heart right before or at birth is not uncommon. It can be emotionally devastating for your loved one.

Privacy Boundaries

ALERT!

Please pay especially careful attention while reading this section. It is an underlying principle of modern adoption practice and should govern your relationship with the adoptee and his family throughout your lives together.

Perhaps one of the more awkward parts of being expectant by adoption is balancing the desire to bring family and friends fully into the process against the importance of respecting the coming child's future privacy and his parents' need for private space right now.

Prospective adopters will weigh carefully how much information to share with their loved ones about possible adoption situations they explore. Though you may not hear about each prospective contact they receive, they will absolutely want to tell you when they have been matched with a pregnant woman and the projected due date, but it is better to share the details of their negotiations and meetings with her only with their adoption counselors. If they are adopting internationally, you can certainly expect that they will be pleased as punch to share that fuzzy referral picture of the child they accept, though they will be less forthcoming about sharing the detailed written report that accompanies it. Why is this?

The unique concept of bringing together the needs and the desires of two sets of parents (most often previously unknown to one another) on behalf of the greater needs of a child is a huge task. No matter whether the birth and adoptive parents will meet one another and forge an ongoing relationship or they will choose confidentiality, a great deal of very intimate information will change hands. Far more often than not adopting parents will have access to significant medical and social information about their child. They may learn details about family background or social history. They may have access to information about the birthfamily's medical history and mental health problems and learning disabilities. The story occasionally includes difficult details about rape, or incest, or infidelity, or imprisonment, or substance abuse.

This is very private stuff.

It may be difficult for you to understand completely, but please accept the fact that, curious as you may be (usually with the very best of intentions) your adopting loved one will have been cautioned by the professionals helping with the adoption to share as little as possible about these details with family members and friends.

One of the key tasks of adoptive parenting that makes it different from parenting a child born to the family is talking to the child about his personal story. Adoptive parents are encouraged to teach their growing children the difference between secrecy (usually shame based) and privacy. As he grows, the child will begin to learn how to exercise good judgment about what to tell and to whom.

There are a number of reasons for this emphasis on privacy. First, there is the issue of ownership. *This information belongs exclusively to the child.* It really isn't his adopting parents' to share with you. Some of it may need to be shared with physicians or therapists, and in the future all of it will be imparted to the child (in age-appropriate bites). Second, there is the concern about gossip. Keeping confidences is hard, and most confidences are broken. Private information once shared can never be retrieved. A piece of information shared privately is shared with one more, who shares it with yet one more person. Eventually, everyone who knows forgets that the information was ever confidential and it becomes family gossip. When this has happened, sometimes the child overhears from others information about himself to which he has not yet been made privy. He feels embarrassed and perhaps betrayed by his parents. Not good.

It's best that this information stay within the adopters' own household. Please understand that his should not be interpreted as an unwillingness to be forthcoming with you, but instead it should be seen as respectful of the child and his birthfamily's right to privacy. Be prepared to honor and respect the adopted person's privacy throughout his lifetime.

Pregnant by Adoption

Treat waiting adopters as expectant—giggle and fuss! Maree remarked "If I were six months pregnant, people would be drooling over me, but since I'm expecting by adoption, I get so much nonchalance, shock, and plain old rudeness. Adoption is sometimes treated as not being 'real' (and, of course, with all the hopes and fears, some of us hold back in our excitement) therefore, it would be helpful for those around us to understand our need to be treated as if we are expecting, or pregnant by adoption."

If there was a physical pregnancy would you be frightening your child with pregnancy loss stories? Beth felt that her family was doing just this, "Optimistic outlooks from friends and family would have been a really big help for us. My mother-in-law was a constant worry-out-loud type, very pessimistic. After a while it just made me angry with her, like maybe she didn't really think adoption was a good idea."

Though most of us think only of the primary definition of the word *pregnant*— "carrying a developing fetus within the uterus"—the word has other usages as well. According to The *American Heritage Dictionary of the English Language*, the adjective *pregnant* also means "creative; inventive; fraught with significance; abounding; overflowing; filled; charged." Certainly, to be expecting a child—whether by birth or by adoption—is fraught with significance, charged with emotion, and necessitates creative and inventive thinking and actions.

Those who have completed a parent preparation process and are awaiting a traditional agency placement or who have been matched with a birthfamily who has chosen them as prospective parents for a coming child have every right to consider themselves pregnant in several senses of the word. And being pregnant is far from a static event. It's all about getting ready to take on an all new role—that of parent to a particular child who is going to be born and need the nurturing attention of at least one parent in infancy and through childhood and into adulthood, by a parent or parents whom he will carry within himself (even after their deaths) for all of his own life.

Physical pregnancy is such a concrete event that it creates an opportunity not just for the mother-to-be, but for her partner and for her family and friends to begin to anticipate and prepare emotionally and in practical ways for the arrival of a new person in their inner circle. It provides, as well, the opportunity for women friends and family to begin to "mentor" new mothers, drawing them into a "sisterhood" of shared knowledge and support that most take very much for granted.

The psychological changes that take place for both mothers and fathers during a pregnancy are every bit as important as are the physical changes a pregnant woman experiences. During the nine months that biological parents wait for birth, both expectant mothers and involved expectant fathers become introspective, communicating with one another and their baby in a rich and slowly growing joint fantasy, while sharing with one another common fears and anxieties. Waiting for a baby to arrive—no matter how carefully planned and no matter how much he was wanted— nearly always involves ambivalence. And while they sort through this ambiguity, pregnant parents begin the practical steps of nest building: creating physical and emotional space in their homes and in their lives as they grow to love the particular child whose birth they are awaiting.

There are actually many parallels between being expectant by adoption and being pregnant. You can learn more about these parallels if you wish by reading. I got a wonderful note via e-mail from a dad-to-be who had stumbled upon *Adopting after Infertility* on his own while in the midst of his homestudy and was trying to read it sandwiched between the required reading from his agency. He wrote, "BTW, when I read the section on psychological pregnancy I got so excited that I wanted to re-decorate the spare bedroom—at 11:30 at night. More and more, raising a child seems to be an immediate reality and not some nebulous event in the hazy future. I think we've taught ourselves not to raise our hopes, so it almost took someone else's permission for us to hope again."

Is it time for a shower? New adoptive parents need "stuff" too! Besides, the concept of a shower is not just to provide gifts, but also to provide a warm welcome to the new community member. Adopting parents need to feel that they "belong" to the parenting world. Now, while they are expecting, your kids need your support. A psychological pregnancy should also involve the adopters' circle of family and friends in the rituals common to preparing for a new baby—nursery preparation, layette gathering, baby showers. These rituals are a routine part of Role Transition for those who are physically pregnant, and those who are preparing to launch a baby's adoption should actively create a similar situation for expectant adopters.

Some hospitals, adoptive parent groups, or infertility support groups offer adoption "Lamaze" classes (often based on

Carol Hallenbeck's *Our Child: Preparation for Parenting in Adoption* curriculum guide). Such classes are a supplement to, rather than an extension of, a homestudy. They offer practical guidance and transitional emotional support in a kind of initiation ritual for prospective adopting parents. The classes cover such topics as choosing a pediatrician, bathing and other basic infant care issues, feeding (exploring both adoptive nursing and bottle feeding), product selection, managing day-to-day, etc. If you r children can't find such a class in their community, encourage them consider asking an appropriate sponsor to offer one.

Karen wrote that when she was unable to find such a class available when her son arrived unannounced, she called the local hospital and found, "The childbirth educator there was thrilled to give us a private infant care class. She gave us lots of valuable information about newborns that we probably would not have known otherwise."

Health Care for Expectant Adopters

One of the things that adoptive parents worry about is whether their child-to-be's birthmother has had good prenatal care. Adopters' concerns are for the most part focused on the baby's need for a healthy pre-natal environment free of toxins, alcohol, recreational drugs and unnecessary medications. One of the remnants of lost family-planning control that rises insistently to the surface while adopters wait for their child to come home to them is that they can do very little to insure that he is nurtured by a mother's healthy eating and sleeping and exercise regimen. At the same time, many birthmothers have very strong feelings about taking good care of the babies for whom they are considering an adoption plan. They speak frequently about how powerful it makes them feel to know that, while they don't feel that they will be able to adequately parent their children over the long haul, they feel wonderful about being able to do the healthy things that will get him off to the best possible start.

But good prenatal care is not only about the needs of babies. New fathers and, yes, new adoptive parents, too, need to be in the best possible physical condition when a new child arrives. Babies are demanding little creatures whose needs for food and dry diapers and cuddling and comforting rarely occur only during the day at the beginning. The arrival of a new baby (or toddler or older child) is nearly always accompanied by weeks and even months of sleep deprivation as the caregiver dozes with one ear open for the sounds of a restless baby and the little one deals with his change of environment and establishes both trust with his caretakers and a familiar and comforting routine in his new home.

The inability to follow one's usual routine with any predictability adds to the physical and emotional stress of new parenthood. Meals may be skipped when a caregiver tries to meet a baby's demands and then uses the baby's quiet times to "catch up" with mounting laundry or cleaning or to snatch a short nap. Even experienced parents may question their parenting skills with a baby whose basic temperament is fussy and demanding.

New parents of older babies often complain about strained muscles and unexpected physical exhaustion. Remember, a pregnant woman gradually adjusts to increases in the amount of weight she carries before the baby is born, and her muscular structure changes with the growing baby, while adoptive parents are suddenly carrying nine pounds of extra weight along with a grocery sack, or juggling a fifteen pound four-month-old in a front carrier while pushing a vacuum cleaner, or making much more frequent trips up a flight of stairs with extra human baggage in tow.

Marie was single and 45 when her daughter arrived from China at nine months of age. Never much for exercising, she was already dealing with arthritis in an area of her lower back injured in an accident many years before. Within days of LiAnne's arrival Marie had badly strained herself, causing her doctor to recommend that she not lift her child for several weeks. This complicated Marie's caretaking abilities and confused her daughter's emotional need for consistent care and nurturing body contact from her only parent. Marie was grateful for help from her mother and her sister-in-law, but she was disappointed by her own lack of preparation which resulted in her less than full participation in her daughter's early adjustment. Marie was thrilled to be able to offer her experience as a cautionary tale for readers of this book and to recommend establishing an early workout routine as a part of getting ready for parenthood!

Getting ready for a new baby, then, involves getting new parents' bodies ready, too. An adoptive pregnancy should involve a regular exercise program that includes strengthening exercises for the lower back, arms, and legs. An informed caring friend or family member could have subtly influenced Marie's situation for the better. Offer yourself as a regular exercise partner for an expectant adopter. He or she may be stressed out and distracted and so you may have to push just a little. *You* find the class or the program and get the two of you signed up. *You* get written into your friend's calendar. *You* call with scheduling reminders and provide transportation if necessary. Make it easy for this person to take the opportunity to get into shape and relax at the same time!

Parents-to-be who have not learned relaxation techniques before should consider taking a yoga class or a stress reduction workshop or investing in some meditation tapes in order to be ready for one of parenthood's guaranteed requirements—needing to remain calm in the face of a crying baby's refusal to be comforted. Might you, as grandparents-to-be offer the gift of such a class or a health club membership to your expectant children?

Since non-parents are particularly at risk for skipping meals, eating on the run, and treating their own nutrition lightly, adopters should use this waiting time to start new eating habits that will not only make them feel better during the early months of their child's life, but also with serve as a foundation for learning to feed a son or daughter healthy foods on a regular schedule and establishing the healthy family ritual of mealtimes together. Waiting adopters are under psychological stress during this waiting period, and so their bodies are particularly susceptible to the effects of poor eating habits. They may want to use this time to stop smoking (it will be far easier now than during the stressful period of adapting to parenthood); eliminate alcohol; eat less salt and sugar and red meat and more fruits and vegetables. They will need your support for this, but try to avoid nagging.

Women who are physiologically pregnant are more or less forced by their changing bodies to slow their lives down. They tire easily and, as time goes by, move more slowly. By association their involved partners slow down too, and this forced slowing down and paring back—working fewer hours, giving up some social and volunteer commitments, staying home more—makes space for the reveries of transition. Adopting parents must force themselves to make these choices. In getting ready to become a parent—for the first or the second or third time—parents must readjust their lives. The waiting period provides the right time for making those adjustments. Couples who are pregnant-by-adoption and are caught up in the need to get space ready for a baby's arrival, or who are working on the paperwork needed to travel to another country, must give themselves permission to adjust their lifestyles. Once again, the invisibility of an adoption "pregnancy" may make it difficult for family and friends to recognize the purpose behind waiting parents' deliberate slowing down and turning inward. Your support of this process can make a huge difference.

The Sympathetic Pregnancy

Adopters sometimes have pregnancy "symptoms." I'm kidding, right? Nope!

It's long been realized, but continues to be infrequently talked about, that over 60% of the male partners of pregnant women experience symptoms that seem to mirror some of those felt by their physiologically pregnant spouses. Expectant fathers report food cravings followed by weight gain, sleep disturbances, back pain, and even the frequent urination usually caused in pregnant women by the pressure of her growing uterus on her bladder. In an interview for my book *Launching a Baby's Adoption*, adoption educator Sharon Kaplan Roszia noted something even less often discussed: that in her 30+ years of experience with adopting couples she's often seen prospective adopters who appear to be experiencing phenomena she refers to as "sympathetic symptoms of pregnancy." One or both partners may experience repeated, and even predictably scheduled, episodes of nausea. Food cravings and significant weight gain are not unusual. One or both may complain of sleep disturbances or emotional peaks and valleys.

When talking about expectant fathers with pregnant wives, counselors usually explain these symptoms as fathers' subconscious attempts to become part of the pregnancy. Of course, to a certain extent there may be some more concrete explanations, as well. For example, pregnant women usually try to eat more healthily and are even encouraged to eat more calories than before. The resulting change in Mom-to-be's diet may spill over via the menu of what's served and what's available to munch on to Dad. Changes in diet can cause changes in bowel and bladder habits. Nervous anticipation could cause an upset stomach. Natural ambivalence about the impending role change and its resulting responsibilities heightens emotional reactions. A restless partner in one's bed often disturbs one's own sleep.

I'll bet that most readers of this book had never thought about adopters going through a similar change, but it's true! There are logical psychological and physiological explanations for real physical symptoms of sympathetic pregnancy experienced by some prospective adopters. If a subconscious reason for a man whose partner is physiologically pregnant to experience sympathetic symptoms might be his subconscious yearning to be a part of the pregnancy, could not this explain why expectant adoptive parents feel similar symptoms? The tension of the wait, often exacerbated by worries that something will happen and/or a lack of support from family and friends, not to mention the suddenly heightened awareness that society in general doesn't have particularly positive attitudes about adoption can create many physical problems. Nausea can be tension-related. Under stress people often snack more often or partake of "comfort foods" or experience cravings—all of which can lead to weight gain. Changes in weight often make us feel both physically uncomfortable—clothing too tight, pressure on the bladder, just not "up to par"—and psychologically stressed. Any of the above stressors may lead to sleep disturbances. The heightened anxiety of all of these pending changes and challenges sets many people on edge and triggers sudden emotional responses.

Just as one cannot predict with certainty whether a pregnant woman or her partner will experience any of these side effects of a physiological pregnancy, it is impossible to predict whether one or both partners in a pregnant-by-adoption couple might be prone to these symptoms. Knowing they could appear, though, allows us to understand such symptoms as "normal" if they do appear, and to offer the stress-reducing support that is so important.

Nesting

With the adoption decision made and the homestudy/parent preparation process completed, prospective parents should find that they want to begin nest-building behaviors. They will begin by evaluating how a child will fit into their physical space. Has the living space been designed with adults-only in mind? If so, expectant parents may find it easier to make adjustments or make a move before their child arrives rather than waiting until both parents and baby must be uprooted several months down the road. In adoption, this can be an even more important thing to consider, so that a child who has already made more transitions of "home" and "parents" than most other children does not have to deal with yet another change.

The coming child needs a quiet sleeping space, storage for his paraphernalia, and eventually his own room. Serious child-proofing could wait until he's mobile, but beginning to think about their home as a place where babies may crawl, toddlers may explore, etc., will help to make plans for the expanding family. This may be true for grandparents-to-be as well.

In the absence of any visible signs of pregnancy, visiting a children's furniture store can feel strange at first, and the support of a grandma-to-be or about-to-be-aunt who has already been through the expectant parent process accomplishes a number of good things. Acknowledging the reality of the coming child and providing a supportive mentoring experience send the clear message that it's OK to get caught up in the excitement generated by the pretty things in the store, and that you, as future family to the coming adoptee, are excited by the process, too.

Adoptive parents' needs are the same as are those of parents expecting to give birth. Baby will need a car seat, a bed, a place to store clothes, feeding and changing equipment. Selecting these things and having them placed in the family home claims space for a child there. But of course, for those who simply can't make the leap of faith (and in some cultures even pregnant parents don't buy these things in advance), the next best thing to purchasing is to do the shopping and either store them at the home of a friend or family member (yours?) or to keep a list of where to find everything when they are at least needed.

The waiting period finds many would-be moms and dads beginning to read and learn about parenting—parenting in general as well as parenting by adoption. A nice gift from supportive grandparents might be the purchase of some good adoptive parenting books—titles like *Raising Adopted Children* (Melina) or *Parenting Your Adopted Child* (Siegel) or *Launching a Baby's Adoption* (Johnston) or *Toddler Adoption* (Hopkins-Best) or *Inside Transracial Adoption* (Steinberg and Hall)—and it can be even more satisfying now to focus *not* on the adoption aspect of the transition to parenthood, but on the normal, everybody-does-it practicalities found in the What-to-Expect series or Dr. Spock or T. Berry Brazelton..

Encourage the waiting adopters to stretch to the extent that they are able, but to do only the nesting things that make them comfortable. Browse with them in the baby section at department stores. Look through the baby books and baby announcements at the card store. Ask about giving them a shower. Don't push and shove, however. Try your best to understand the ambivalence and hesitancy that can accompany an adoptive pregnancy and the fact that this, too, could fail them.

While waiting for Brandon to arrive, Denise was sometimes overwhelmed with frustration because there was no time frame. She wrote, "I found that knitting a baby blanket, working out on a treadmill, and nurturing myself really prepared me for my son. Interviewing a few pediatricians and taking an adoptive parenting class was really helpful, too."

Couples planning an open adoption may have practical opportunities to involve themselves in a prospective birthmother's pregnancy, visiting the obstetrician with her, watching her belly grow, feeling the baby kick, attending birthing classes. Their extended family members tend to find this frightening. While your hesitancy is understandable—particularly since you have not had the opportunity to learn as much about adoption and openness as the adopters' have, your family members need you to trust that they know what they are doing here. Many adopters find that a psychological pregnancy is much easier for them when the concrete evidence of a coming child provided by contact with his birthmother is a part of their every day lives, but those who are planning confidential or international adoptions can and should give themselves the opportunity to feel expectant, too.

One of the complications common to international adoption is that children sometimes "age up" while red tape is sorted through. It is not unusual for families to receive a referral several months before they actually travel to unite parents and child. These delays can be particularly stressful, as families struggle with their feelings of powerlessness, fret about whether their child is receiving adequate care, and worry about possible complications. Among the practical things parents can do to make the best use of such a wait and at the same time strengthen their sense of connection with their child is to begin learning about normal infant development during each of the weeks and months until parents and child are together forever. Families with this kind of wait may want to read books on baby's first year. One easy way to do this is to subscribe to the newsletter *Growing Child*, from Dunn & Hargitt Publishers, West Lafayette, Indiana. A subscription to *Growing Child* begins by supplying the publisher with a child's sex, name, and birth date. Beginning immediately, parents begin to receive monthly newsletters that correspond to their particular child's age that particular month. So that, for example, the newsletter received when the child is three months old will describe the kinds of physical, emotional, cognitive development that is within the range of normal for children four months old. Each issue offers advice about problems common to that particular age and stage of development (sleeping through the night, or using a pacifier, or stranger anxiety, or pulling up, or finding his fingers, for example) and offers suggested exercises and activities parents can try, and information about appropriate toys and games. *Growing Child* makes clear that the range of "normal" is a wide one, but will offer parents an opportunity for developing a relatively realistic picture of what their child may be like as he waits to come to them. Looking for a "waiting" gift for the family who has accepted the referral of a child born half way across the world? Consider *Growing Child*!

After attending one of my workshops, Roni Breite wrote about her experience with a psychological pregnancy in the RESOLVE of Greater San Diego newsletter. She described her decisions to buy books for her child-to-be, to tell members of her family (especially nieces and nephews who, as children, tended to be much more positive than their own parents), collecting potential names, cleaning out a room (but Roni wasn't quite brave enough to fill it up again). She wrote

"Sure, my expectancy is tenuous and invisible to most of the world—hidden, in fact, at work. It's tainted by the learned anticipation of failure. And my expectancy isn't really our expectancy. Sometimes I think it's just a mind game I play to keep my spirits up, a game my husband, my rock, my angel, doesn't need to or want to play... But I remind myself that it is a legitimate, important step in making the transition from childlessness to parenting, so I continue to indulge, tentatively, cautiously.

"It helps me believe."

📖 Learn more about it:

Launching a Baby's Adoption by Patricia Irwin Johnston
(Perspectives Press, Inc., 1998)

They're back?

As they begin to enjoy a psychological pregnancy, adopters
are likely to begin to feel less resistant to other people's children
than they did when they were childless or feeling infertile. This
can be an awkward transition for many friends and family members. Especially when the parent-to-be has come to adoption out
of infertility, they may have been very difficult to live with. After
having had to mute the joy in their own family building and bite
their tongues when feeling impatient with childless family members who were either disinterested in nieces and nephews, down-
right jealous about them, or who remained removed entirely
from the expanding new generation of their family, some brothers and sisters and cousins and friends of these folks find it hard
to make an about-face.

Someone has to take a first step. Could it be you? I encourage you to keep in mind that those "other people" who seemed
so difficult to be with were not behaving in character. They were
mourning—silently—but truly. Can you find it in your heart to
try to reach out to them and welcome them back to the family
fold? The results will be worth your while! Including sensitive
and patient family and closest friends in the adoption process
brings them along with the new parents in the same way that
watching a sister's belly bloom brings a family along throughout
her pregnancy.

Some prospective parents like "borrowing" babies for short
stretches by babysitting for family or friends for a few hours or

by volunteering in their church or synagogue nursery or toddler rooms. Waiting adopters may observe children more closely in public places, noticing different textures of hair, different skin tones, different body shapes, different personality types and fantasizing about how the coming child may look. You may tend to do this too!

Practical Preparation—Expecting by Adoption

Whatever you feel comfortable doing to help your family members during the waiting period will be very much appreciated. At the very least be prepared to offer them patient moral support. Keep in mind that asking "how it's going" too frequently can become particularly irritating to would-be parents who are already feeling frustrated and anxious about the plodding pace of their adoption.

Families "expecting by adoption" face the same practical and emotional tasks as do those who are pregnant. They must begin to get their bodies, their hearts, their homes, and their families ready for the arrival of a very dependent new person.

Defining the practical things that must be done is the easiest part:

1. Is the house or apartment ready for a child? Is there room for bed, dresser and clothes, toys, age-appropriate paraphernalia? If not, the time to move is before the child arrives.

2. What financial accommodations must be made? Will they be operating on one less income? If not, can the family afford for one or both parents to take some parenting leave while the family adjusts? Childcare must be arranged.

What about life insurance for the new parents? How about wills? Guardianship?

3. Adjustments must be made to the family schedule. Will work hours need adjustment or accommodation? Should volunteer commitments be changed or eliminated?

4. An adoption-aware pediatrician or family doctor must be interviewed and selected.

5. If the child will be older, there may be a need for special school arrangements, for counseling, for therapists, for foreign language translators. Compiling this list ahead of time is a good idea.

6. It's important that new parents get themselves into the best possible physical shape. Whether the new arrival is a newborn, a toddler or a ten year old, sleeping and eating patterns will be disrupted, schedules will be changed. New parents most often find themselves lifting and carrying weights their backs may not be used to.

A freezer stocked with food or deliveries of fully prepared meals will be much appreciated. How about the gift of a month's laundry service or a cleaning service? Volunteering *not* to care for the child—that's the new mom or dad's job—but instead to take up the slack in other areas that need doing will offer important support.

If you have a skill, share it with this family. As soon as possible after your loved ones announce that an adoption is in the offing, get thee to thy woodshop or sewing room and make something special for this new family member, something that will become part of his own collection of family heirlooms. And, speaking of heirlooms, don't wait to be asked about the use of an heirloom rocker or cradle or baptismal dress—offer it immediately to demonstrate your recognition that this child will be a *real* member of the family.

These suggestions have not been an exhaustive list, but they provide a good start for friends or family members looking for ways in which they can personally help to support the expanding family financially or practically.

Home at Last!

Naming as Claiming

> "What's in a name? That which we call a rose by any other name would smell as sweet" –William Shakespeare, Romeo and Juliet, Act II, Scene 2

What will the baby be named? Would-be parents often begin thinking about this when they are little kids fantasizing about being grownups. So now Mom-and-Dad-to-be spend months and months pouring over a collection of names-for-the-baby books borrowed from the library or picked up in the check out line at the grocery story. Mom one that's not "too ordinary." Her partner wants one that won't be "too different." It needs to sound right with the agreed upon surname. They try a few out on friends and relatives (like you!) and watch their faces for reactions... "Oh, isn't that unUSual, dear."... "How interesting!"... "Cute." ... "Pretty big name for a little tiny person, isn't it?" ... "That's nice, and you can call him _____?"

Let's be honest. Naming is indeed a big deal for most families. Most of us carry our names with us from birth to the grave, we are identified by them, and they are a part of our own self-identity. How we wear our own names even directly influences how others come to feel about the name in general, not just us as individuals—a factor that influences what names we ourselves "like" when thinking about names for our children. For most parents, carefully choosing a name that has family or cultural significance or sounds pleasing to their ears is an important way to "claim" their child and is seen as a "right" of parenting. In many cultures and religions around the world the public calling out of a name shortly after a child's arrival carries profound significance.

For adoptive parents, however, the issue of naming a child may feel complicated and extended family members need to become attuned to these complications. In making one's own a child who has another set of relatives by birth and a genetic heritage different from that of his adoptive family, important questions are raised.

- Should the two sets of parents (birth and adoptive) agree on a name in an open adoption, or is the naming the right of one or the other set of parents?

- Should Kim Soon Hee or Marushka Wiscznowski keep all or part of names that reflect the culture and ethnicity of their countries of birth or should their names be "Americanized," and, if changed, might the change be interpreted as disrespectful of the culture of origin?

- Might it be a burden or is it a blessing for a child not genetically related to his family to bear a name rich in family heritage—Reynaud Leviathan Fitzsimmons Curtis IV?

- What about the family already parenting a son who fall in love with a toddler in the photo-listing book whose first name is the same (George I and George 2?— Hey, the famous boxing Foreman family did it on purpose!)

There are no easy answers to this particular list of questions. Depending on the unique circumstances of the families involved in each baby's adoption, decisions about ethnicity and names, or passing along names with strong family meanings, or dealing with name duplication appropriately may differ from one family to the next. But there are some things that they will think about…

Child development experts have presumed for years that babies younger than seven months old were not really aware of their own names. Recent research at the State University of New York at Buffalo, however, offers some interesting new data. Psychologist Peter Jusczyk and his team observed how long infants looked toward a stereo speaker that played four different prerecorded names. The results were that babies as young as four and a half months focused on the speaker an average of four seconds longer when their own names were played.

According to Jusczyk, when a baby learns to recognize her name it is the first intellectual sign that she is beginning to attach meaning to the sounds she hears. And name recognition is an important social milestone, too. It is, says Jusczyk, "One main step on the way toward a child developing a sense of self."

For children adopted at ages older than infancy, the issue of changing a name is generally acknowledged to be significant, and most adoption professionals discourage changing names of older children without careful thought and consultation. Psychologists agree that unless a child is carefully prepared and follow up is conscientious, changing the first name of a child beyond the second half of his second year of life (by which time he has comes to internalize it) carries the risk that the child may subconsciously presume that the old name and the person who bore it were "bad" and "rejectable." For such children bearing a new name that makes him feel like an imposter may create a struggle to be "good," but not authentic. On the other hand, some older aged adoptees may specifically request that their names be changed in order to make them feel less "different" in their new environments or to facilitate their own feelings of entitlement toward the family. Though a few parents continue to discard their internationally adopted child's original name, more and more now feel that, no matter what his age at arrival, it is important to celebrate and honor his ethnic background by keeping at least a portion of his original name, often as a middle name.

Adoption grows families, and in child-centered adoptions what's best for the child must take precedence over the wishes and needs of the adults in his life. The issue of naming the child is one of the significant differences in adoption-expanded families that deserves careful, well-informed thought and action on everyone's part.

> "What's in a name? That is what we ask ourselves
> in childhood when we write the name that we are
> told is ours."   — James Joyce, *Ulysses.*

Arrival Issues

For his parents, one of the most challenging aspects of the actual arrival of your long-awaited grandchild will be coping with the tumult! After months of being oh-so-ready, arrival can sometimes become mass confusion. The excitement of others often tends to produce too much of a good thing.

When parents give birth there are certain expectations related to the physical process of giving birth which produce much needed support for the family. The physical experience of labor and delivery has been a strain, so there is the expectation that Mom will be sore and tired. She is usually given some resting space. Traditionally in many families grandparents arrive to help with housekeeping so that Mother and Baby can have time alone. As times have changed and extended family members have become more and more likely to live at some distance and/or to have jobs which make their participation difficult, some families have hired doulas (women whose supportive role might be compared to that of a midwife, but who offer their assistance after the birth) for this purpose. Friends bring or send in meals or offer to run errands.

When families adopt—and even more often when they adopt a child who is not newborn—these supportive steps are often left out. They shouldn't be! If your daughter had given birth, wouldn't you go to help? Why? Not just because she would be recovering from a physical trauma, but also because this is a way that families claim each other. Mothers and mothers-in-law teach their sons and daughters about parenting. Don't deny yourself or your son and daughter or your grandchild this same experience just because they are adopting! Tell your loved ones in advance that you would like to help in whatever way you can. Ask to be part of their joy.

But, a word of caution is in order here. It is not uncommon for adopting parents to experience what I've come to call a Cinderella syndrome, finding themselves cooking and cleaning for visiting guests who are delighted to come and visit the new baby, but who have overlooked or forgotten how much of new parents' exhaustion after a new child's arrival has to do with the lack of sleep and adaptation to massive change as much as it has to do with the recovery from having given birth, and so they behave as guests. Don't allow this to happen in your family. There are several things you can do in the months in advance of your grandchild's arrival to prepare to deal with or prevent Cinderella Syndrome...

- Prepare and freeze some main dishes for the microwave, or collect restaurant take-out menus and set aside budgeted money for extra help with the new parents' meals.
- Offer professional assistance with housecleaning during the first weeks after arrival.

Before the child arrives, speak to the expectant parents about their projected needs and wishes for arrival week and let them take the lead, finding ways to include yourself which will not deplete their energies. Obviously they want their extended family to claim their child as their own, but they may find it awkward to encourage this while at the same time dealing with their nuclear family's needs. You need to acknowledge and be patient about this. If the new family lives nearby, this may be easier to accomplish than if they live in other cities, as you will be able to limit and stagger visiting times. If you will be visiting from out of town, discuss with your family before arrival time what arrangements will need to be made. Would they prefer that you stay in a hotel this time? Can you be helpful to them in other ways as they attend to their new child's physical and emotional needs (an important step in forging attachment between new parents and child)? Might it be better to send snapshots or videotapes via Internet or overnight mail for family members to view on arrival day and then to speak frequently by phone for the first week or so before planning for you to come for a visit? What do they want?

These early days and weeks are precious times for families. Striking a balance between protecting the family's privacy and including others in their joy is an issue of balance to wrestle with—the first of many that accompany parenthood. The new family needs your support, rather than your criticism or hurt feelings as they work to strike this balance.

Circling the Wagons

Part of the process of claiming a new family member and forming attachments involves what I call "circling the wagons" and some others have called "cocooning." To one extent or another, nearly all families, no matter how they are formed, create

an almost ritualized time and space for shutting off the outside
world and allowing only immediate family members access to a
new baby and his parents. Wagon circling is healthy behavior,
and it is rarely questioned—or even noticed—by most non-fam-
ily members, who seem to take such behavior pretty much for
granted—especially in families built by birth.

When a new baby arrives, grandparents and aunts and uncles
close ranks with new parents, using their experience "when you
were little" to teach the new generation how to care for "one of
us." As families share expertise and experience ("Remember when
our sister Sherry was born, and..." or "Gosh, he has long fingers
just like Jonathan's!") they reinforce the intimate web that binds
the family together.

For adoption-expanded families, wagon circling may carry
even more significance than it does for families extended by birth.
Arrival is a time during which all members of a family are finally
brought face-to-face with any remaining fears they may have
had about attaching between parents and child and about extended family members' willingness and ability to embrace the
new family member as "one of our own." This baby is not likely
to "look like" someone in the family, but similar experiences of
feeling awkward in handling a child or in feeling sleep deprived
or in experiencing the natural "what have we gotten ourselves
into" ambivalence common to nearly all new parents draw family members together to support one another.

Since the process of adoption has often put exceptional stress
on parents-to-be, who have often found their families to be less
helpful in offering them support than have their support group
friends who have "been there," creating a special moment in time
for cocooning and family claiming sends important messages
from everyone in a family to everyone else. New parents hear
the message that their child is accepted, and that they are seen to
be "real" parents just as are family members who have given birth.

Extended family members hear the message that their connections to the new family are important and expected and desired.

The older the child at arrival, the more likely it is that early visits from family and friends which are more than a few hours in length will not serve the family's immediate needs. In fact, don't be surprised if, in advance of the placement, your loved ones take the advice I offer in *Launching a Baby's Adoption* and informs local friends, co-workers and neighbors of their need to have quiet, private time together for a few days before opening themselves to visitors. Please don't allow yourself to be offended by this need. Instead, support it! A practical way to handle this is for the new parents to let everyone know that they will be holding an open house on a weekend afternoon a week or two after the child's arrival. The family may suggest to you or others close to them that arranging for refreshments and/or helping with preparation and cleanup for this open house would be a welcome and much appreciated baby gift. Dive in!

Some families arrange for their telephone to be answered by machine for a week or more. The message might announce the news and explain that the chaos of settling in prevents them from taking phone calls or visits for a few days, thanks callers for their congratulations and good wishes, and promises to return their calls as soon as possible.

But wagon-circling can be misinterpreted by three groups of people who may be important to adopting parents and their baby. One group, as discussed above, is their immediate family and long term close friends. A second consists of friends whose bond with the adopters is constructed out of the shared experience of waiting to adopt. If they have been "first" in their group of prospective adopters to welcome their child home, they may find that still-waiting friends are particularly sensitive to anything that makes them feel that they've been forgotten. Concern about this may spill over onto other important relationships.

Also sensitive to the feeling of being "slighted" by wagon-circling behavior are birthparents in open adoptions, who have most often been completely unprepared to feel somehow "excluded" so suddenly. Since wagon circling usually happens very soon after a baby's arrival, birthparents are likely to face it from their baby's adopters at exactly the same time that they are themselves struggling with ambivalence about their adoption plan. They have just begun to react to adoption's grief and loss when suddenly they feel held at arm's length from their baby and his family. Birthparents may even feel some initial panic about having lost not just the baby, but the adopting parents to whom they had become close and on whom they may have become emotionally dependent as well.

The answer is not so simple as to suggest that an entrance be broken open in that circle. This brief window of defensive intimacy can be an important part of attaching. Everyone in the adoption circle needs to be prepared for the wagon circling phenomenon to occur. Adopters need to be aware of it so as not to surprise themselves with it or feel guilty about it and so that they can figure out ways to deal with still waiting friends and with birthparents. Birthparents need to understand in advance that cocooning is not a rejection of themselves and to be helped to see how healthy this kind of claiming is for their child and his new family.

A better solution to the problem is to have discussed this phenomenon in advance and to expect other friends (perhaps other experienced adopters) to provide support to still waiting adopters and the adoption intermediaries to provide support for the baby's birthparents during this special time. With advance notice that wagon circling is going to occur, prospective adopters and birthparents will be better prepared to understand one another's needs and reactions during the first days and weeks after the baby's move to his adoptive home, and can plan in advance how and when their own next contact will occur.

📖 Learn more about it:

Creating Ceremonies: Innovative Ways to Meet Adoption Challenges by Cheryl Lieberman and Rhea Bufferd (Zeig, Tucker and Co, 1999)

The Baby Blues

Post-arrival confusion, anxiety and minor depression is relatively common among new parents. Some sources claim that at least 50% of parents—both fathers and mothers—suffer from the Baby Blues. Unlike the serious medical condition known as postpartum depression, Baby Blues are not necessarily influenced by hormonal fluctuations. That's why it's just as likely that adoptive moms and dads may experience Baby Blues as it is that parents by birth will.

Many factors contribute to the Baby Blues, no matter how the child arrives. Becoming a parent is in itself a major life change. Many parents—including those who have prepared themselves well—initially feel inadequate for such an enormous responsibility when a real baby is finally in their arms. No matter at what age the new child arrives, new parents' sleep patterns are usually interrupted as they sleep with one ear tuned to the needs of a small person in unfamiliar surroundings. Parents may eat differently or even skip meals entirely when distracted by a needy small person. Schedules and routines fall by the wayside. A child who is particularly fussy or anxious, experiencing some attachment difficulties, or is medically needy may create an early parenting experience far different from the idyllic one dreamed of by these new adopters for so long.

Issues specific to adoption may contribute to post-arrival depression, too. Enormous excitement surrounds the arrival of a new member of the family, but what if Mom or Dad is worried that grandparents or aunts and uncles won't accept this child? And what about the insensitive comments ignorant but usually well meaning others throw about? New parents usually take time away from work. Despite recent federal laws which support the need for adoptive parents to have leave, some employers may be less than cooperative if they see post-arrival leave as a medical issue for those who give birth rather than as a parenting issue. Depending on whether your new parent family members were able to plan this well in advance or were surprised by the timing of the adoption, being away from the job can produce anxiety and even guilt—both of which may be enhanced by the parent's berating of self for not being able to forget the job and focus exclusively on the longed-for new arrival.

Some new adopters find that infertility issues resurface briefly when their new child arrives, so that they feel some (usually temporary) sadness that this child is not connected to them genetically. Other adoptive parents are overwhelmed by feelings of sadness for the losses experienced by their child's birthfamily and find it difficult to allow themselves to feel joy rooted in another's grief. Still others find it difficult to let themselves go unconditionally during any period of time when a birthparent's decision may be revoked.

As is often true of those experiencing depressive symptoms, your loved one may need your help in acknowledging that the depression is real and needs to be addressed. You can offer your support by acknowledging that the Baby Blues are normal. Then offer these tips and supports:

- Help these new parents acknowledge that they are only human. That approved homestudy may have felt like getting the Good Housekeeping Seal of Approval, but it didn't grant them status as Super-Parent-To-Be. Don't allow them to beat up on themselves.

- Suggest that the stay-at-home parent should shower and dress before the other parent leaves in the morning. Not only is it hard to find time for this later, but getting off to this kind of "fresh start" can set a tone for the day. Partnerless single parents have a particularly hard time giving themselves these opportunities. Can you be there for that single parent?

- Support their need for eating a balanced diet. (As mentioned before, supportive family members might consider preparing foods for the new family's freezer beforehand or suggesting to friends who want to know what they can do to help that a carried in meal would be welcomed far more than would "holding the baby.")

- Help new parents be kind to their heads and to their souls. Volunteer to be or to hire a sitter to give an overstressed stay-at-home parent a few minutes each day just for himself or herself—to take a leisurely bath, to read a book, to meditate, to make a phone call, etc.

- Volunteer to help new parents relieve stress by becoming their exercise partner and helping them to exercise regularly—yoga stretches during nap time, a brisk walk around the block while pushing a stroller, new parent aerobics or swimming classes (with day care provided) at the local Y.

- Don't allow a new parent to feel "trapped." This can be very hard when you as the caring relative are far away and can't pick up and be there to help. Suggest that the new mom take the baby with her to the mall or a museum or have lunch at Wendy's with a friend. Help them to contact a parents' group.

The Baby Blues are normal, but that doesn't make them seem less scary! Those who find themselves stuck may need help in seeking help, but help is there—from an adoptive parent group, from the child's pediatrician, from the family's social worker, from their family doctor.

Parenting in Adoption

Age at Arrival Issues

Since your new family member may not arrive at his birth, there may be some adjustment problems for the child and his parents. On the other hand, for children who are especially resilient, the transition may go amazingly smoothly. Since it is impossible to predict resiliency, it's best for families to be prepared for the possibility of transition difficulties. These differ, depending upon the child's age at his arrival and his past experiences. You can be of most help in two ways:

- By respecting the professional integrity of those who have prepared and are supporting this child's family. Only if you learn that they do not have supportive adoption resources available to them on an ongoing basis should you consider intervening to offer to help them find those resources..

- By offering unconditional support, including respecting the parenting process and doing nothing to confuse it.

Infancy

Most folks assume that it's pretty easy for new families and adopted babies to adjust—at least easier than making adjustments with older children. Generally, that's true, but there are some important issues to learn about. Psychiatrist Justin Call's research concerning how babies can be expected to react to environmental change at certain vulnerable stages of development during their infancy is, unfortunately, not well known among those who are arranging placements. In a 1974 article called "Helping Infants Cope with Change" published in the January issue of the journal *Early Child Development and Care*, Dr. Call describes how babies of various ages may feel and express distress about a change in environment and caretaker.

Newborns to three-month-old infants are described by Dr. Call as being most concerned with having their needs met. One might assume, then, that if needs continue to be met consistently, babies might not be particularly distressed by changed surroundings. Perhaps, writes Call, this is true of newborns. But it's also true that by age one month, babies are alert enough to respond to stimuli but are not sophisticated enough to modify them, so that until they are over three months old they are susceptible to overstimulation and overload. Call believes that babies who are between four and twelve weeks of age are highly likely to be distressed by a change in environment and caretaker.

A more adaptive time for change is when babies are between three and six months of age. These babies are more able to respond to and modify stimuli, are more adaptive to changes in their environment and are physically sophisticated enough to respond more easily to a changed diet.

But a particularly vulnerable window again appears for the child between six and twelve months of age. Children who have been given the opportunity to do so have usually formed an intense attachment to a caretaker by this time, and if moved they may experience a full range of typical grieving behaviors—shock and denial, anger and despair, depression and withdrawal. It's important to keep in mind that because these losses are occurring before a baby has language with which to communicate directly and successfully, it is hard for him to resolve his anxiety.

Families also need to be prepared for the possibility that a later-arriving infant—even if very healthy—may not have achieved all of the "average" or "normal" milestones when he arrives. Sometimes those delays are a result of Baby's not having had enough one-on-one stimulation in previous environments. In orphanages, babies often have many caretakers in one day and have had no experience learning to rely on one particular adult. Orphanage babies, whose caretakers are often overburdened and busy, may have come to expect few interactions and may not have learned that there can be a cause/effect relationship between expressing a felt need and having it met. Some later-arriving infants may never have experienced comfort and so not know how to accept it. If he has never felt full of food before, never been consistently warm and dry, never felt comforted by cuddling, Baby may have real difficulty understanding these new feelings and accepting them. And if Baby has been deprived of this kind of early caregiving, he may be operating in "survival mode," having become so fearful and stressed as to be hypervigilant. Sometimes developmental delays are traumatically induced regressions that have to do with Baby's fear and discomfort about this move or a series of moves. All of this can be very stressful for new parents—especially those who have not ever parented before. Your patient, loving support is critical at this point.

Every parent wants her child to be as smart as he can be. Adopting parents often worry that the things they've had no control over—a birthmother's poor diet or ingestion of toxins like chemicals or alcohol during her pregnancy, poor nutrition or a lack of stimulation during the period before we become his caregivers, trauma from neglect or abuse or separation—will affect intelligence.

Though basic intelligence is innate, parents who provide appropriate stimulation can offer their babies optimal intellectual support. In the first year babies' brains develop more electronic connections than at any other period in their lives. The first year of life is a crucial one for cognitive development. It behooves new parents to learn as much as they can about where a well-cared-for baby might be expected to be, developmentally, by the time he is the age of their baby at arrival, and to learn as well just how much stimulation a baby of that age can handle. They can then use this information as they interact with the baby and invite extended family to interact as well.

By the middle of the first year of life, babies who have been well stimulated but not over stimulated, who have experienced consistency while being exposed to new things, have been steadily growing cognitively and so are able, on a rudimentary level, to understand that their actions have an effect on the world.

By the end of the first year, most children who have experienced a steady relationship with a trusted caregiver are communicating very well with signals and body language and coos and grunts, and most have begun to use a few words. However, cultural differences and changes of language can create interruptions in this growth, and sometimes these interruptions can trigger regressions.

Progress in motor skills can be delayed as well. Babies whose early months are spent in group care facilities have few of the opportunities for developing motor skills that children cared for by skilled foster parents or reared from the beginning in their adoptive home have. Babies must be unswaddled and given space to learn to kick and to roll from side to side. Children who spend little time being carried but instead spend hours in a crib and then hours strapped in a seat and then more hours in a crib have few opportunities to test their motor skills. If there is nothing colorful or interesting to bat at or try to pick up, Baby may not have learned to grasp a rattle.

Developmentally interrupted children who are given consistent and careful and attentive care and love and stimulation should be expected to catch up within a matter of weeks or months. If Baby does not catch up within a half year of his arrival, her parents will be advised to talk with her doctor about their concerns and elicit help in screening for less common health problems which may have gone unidentified. These could include fetal alcohol syndrome or fetal alcohol effect, lingering effects of institutionalization, undiagnosed post traumatic stress syndrome, etc. Helpful advice may also come from an adoptive parent support group.

If your family member is adopting a child who will not arrive home until he is several weeks or months old, they—and you—can use the time before his placement to get a sense of what milestones he may have passed and what growth experiences he might be expected to have had before he arrives. One way to do this is simply to check out the growth and development books and read the chapters for the weeks and months you will have missed as the child's family. Also consider purchasing a subscription to *Growing Child*, mentioned previously.

Toddlerhood

In her book *Toddler Adoption: The Weaver's Craft*, Mary Hopkins-Best points out that most children who arrive in their new homes at toddler age have not had the opportunity to enjoy consistent parenting from a single loving caregiver, so most toddler adoptions involve significant losses and unique challenges. Those challenges are complicated by the fact that children of this age have neither the spoken language skills nor the thinking and analyzing skills necessary to participate in the kind of talk therapy preparation that can be so helpful to children moving at school age.

Dr. Hopkins-Best writes, "At the precise age when he is beginning to organize his world so that it makes sense and can be acted *upon*, events beyond his control prevent him from doing so. It is no wonder that the single most important development task of his first year of life—learning to *trust*—is undermined or eroded."

What you, as friends and extended family members whose own parenting experience is probably with newborns who grow into toddlerhood in a single stable family, must understand and accept about the new toddler in your world is that the traditional parenting strategies that worked for you are unlikely to work well with the child arriving in toddlerhood. For example, "time outs"—a form of separation and withholding which works so well for the child who has a desire to please and be close to his parents—simply reinforce the poor self concept of the anxious and never-attached toddler and will actually work against their developing healthy attachments.

In most instances (though unfortunately not all) part of the preparation for adoption that families adopting toddler aged children receive involves the opportunity to learn how normal development—emotional, physical, cognitive—can be influenced by the negative early life experiences to which most of these children have been exposed. They will have been taught to expect regression, anger, and grief in their new children as they attach. If the interactions of this family feel "odd" to you, the first step for you to take is to reassure yourself that they have received education, coaching and support specific to toddler adoption.

Your attempts to disrupt what they understand to be important appropriate alternative approaches to parenting such children by doing things differently when the children are with you can undermine the new family. Make it your task to learn as much as you can about how these children can be expected to behave differently from other toddlers and offer your help by supporting this family's consistent approach to parenting, even if it feels strange to you.

Pre-school and elementary school aged kids

There is a clear dividing line for what techniques work with children who are being moved to new homes. That dividing line is the point at which he has the ability to verbalize interactively and the intellectual skills which enable him to separate temporarily from adults to whom he is attached. In her book *A Child's Journey through Placement*, Dr. Vera Fahlberg lists a series of tasks that need to be accomplished by social workers with both prospective parents, prior caretakers, and the children themselves in moving a verbal child from foster care or institutionalization to adoption:

- Introduce the idea of adoption to the child
- Arrange first meetings
- Provide "homework" for the child and family
- Share information
- Get a commitment to proceed
- Plan subsequent pre-placement visits
- Discuss name changes
- Initiate the grief process
- Discuss the "worst of the worst"
- Obtain permission (from prior parent figures) for the child to go and do well
- Facilitate good-byes with foster family, orphanage mates, or others who are important to the child
- Provide ideas for the new family for a welcoming ritual
- Facilitate post-placement contacts
- Arrange for post-placement follow up

The truth is that not all children are moved slowly and carefully and with such attention to detail. In particular, the transitional opportunities of a series of visits before a final move, arrangements for good-byes, and a plan for post-placement contacts are often left out. The result can be confusion and grief for these children. Dr. Fahlberg writes that "the more that the child is aware of considerable communication between the adoptive parent, the foster parent and the caseworker during the pre-placement visits, the more secure he will be. When he knows that everyone knows everything and is comfortable with the information, it relieves him of the fear of saying or doing the wrong thing. The more the child is able to express his mixed feelings about the move, the better. One must remember that no matter how much the child likes the prospective family, he has other feelings—sadness at leaving the family he has learned to love and trust, fear and anxiety about the future, and anger that he has been put in the position of having such confusing emotions."

Again, studies show that most children moved at older ages do very well in their new families. But, after the predictable "honeymoon" period common to adopting older children, families must expect transitional behavior that may feel, at best, different from what they are used to, some developmental regression, and testing behavior. They must expect to be parenting a child who must be supported as he fully experiences the entire cycle of grief and loss (surprise, denial, anger, bargaining, depression, and, finally, resolution).

Parents adopting older children commonly complain that the least helpful thing they hear (repeatedly) from those close to them is, "I told you so. I never understood why you wanted to get yourself into this."

Refrain. Offer instead a hug, a listening ear without responses, an evening's or weekend's respite care (though not unless you are willing to reinforce, rather than undermine, the discipline and structure used by the child's new parents).

Teens

Children placed in "forever homes" as teenagers rarely arrive unbruised. They have often experienced multiple placements—some expected to be temporary and others expected to be permanent—before this one. They can be expected to have self-esteem problems and to have great difficult trusting that adults really mean what they say. They may have been forced to become completely self sufficient or even placed in the role of parent to both themselves and younger or more vulnerable siblings or housemates. Helping such children learn to operate within a healthy family is challenging for everyone. These are kids who have often learned that they can be most successful by playing both ends against the middle. They may try to pit mother against father, siblings against parents, grandparents against parents in their quest for power and control of an out-of-control life. More than anything, the parents of these children need your unwavering support of their absolute position as parents-in-charge. If your new nephew or grandchild arrives at this age more than at any other, your willingness to learn more about it by reading some of the books recommended below will help this family succeed.

The post-institutionalized child

Increasing numbers of children of all ages are being adopted not from family settings (birth, foster, previous adoptive, or even group homes) but from institutions. The older these children are at arrival, the more complex may be their adjustment. Institutionalization provides no experience with one-on-one relationships, involves little verbal interaction, demands that needs be met not as felt but on caretaker's schedule, etc. Such children have often been understimulated during the most crucial times in the development of their brains and may thus experience serious delays and problems with learning as well as with behavior control. Unless they are very resilient, these children can be very troubled. Few American medical, counseling, and educational professionals have had enough experience with such children to understand how to diagnose and treat the problems common to children who have been institutionalized. They are unique. The Parent Network for the Post-Institutionalized Child (http://www.pnpic.org) is a national parent group focused just on these issues and can serve as a first-call line of support and referral for families dealing with the aftereffects of institutionalization.

📖 Learn more about it:

The resources in this section have been arranged in sequence according to the ages of the children they discuss...

International Adoption: Challenges and Opportunities edited by Thais Tepper, Lois Hannon, and Dorothy Sandstrom (Parent Network for the Post-Institutionalized Child, second edition, 2000)

Launching a Baby's Adoption by Patricia Irwin Johnston (Perspectives Press, Inc., 1998)

Toddler Adoption: The Weaver's Craft by Mary Hopkins-Best (Perspectives Press, Inc., 1997)

With Eyes Wide Open: A Workbook for Parents Adopting International Children by Margi Miller and Nancy Ward (Children's Home Society of Minnesota, LN Press, 1996)

Helping Children Cope With Separation and Loss by Claudia Jewett Jarratt (Harvard Common Press, rev. 1994)

A Child's Journey through Placement by Vera Fahlberg, M.D. Perspectives Press, Inc., 1991)

Adopting the Hurt Child by Gregory C. Keck and Regina Kopecky

Can This Child Be Saved? Solutions for Adoptive and Foster Families by Foster Cline M.D. and Cathy Helding (World Enterprises, 1999)

Help for the Hopeless Child: Special Discussion for Assessing and Treating the Post-Institutionalized Child by Ronald S. Federici, M.D. (Jason Aronson, 1998)

Adoption Issues through a Lifetime

No matter whether they joined their families as newborns or as teens, for those who have been adopted, the fact of adoption is and will be part of who they are throughout their lives. Some may think about adoption very little, while for others their adoption may become an obsession, but whether an adopted person finds himself at one end of such a continuum or the other or somewhere in the middle, adoption will be there, part of the fabric of what makes them who they are, forever. We know that there are certain adoption-related issue likely to come up at particular phases of life. This section introduces those, and must start with an important concept for you to try your best to understand. That concept is that, though many parents and grandparents and aunts and uncles are threatened to some extent by the idea that a beloved adoptee could have any "issues" they need not be. These normal developmental issues for a person who was adopted nearly always simply reconfirm the "realness" of his relationship with the family who adopted him.

In Infancy and Toddlerhood

At this stage, the issues are far more likely to be the family's rather than the child's. This is a time when the immediate and extended families get used to the prying questions of others, and the comments that seem to question the family's validity. Often these are comments they may have made themselves before, but now that they've come to be personally touched by adoption, adoptive parents and grandparents and aunts and uncles find hurtful such remarks as

"Why did they *have to* adopt?"

"Do you know anything about his *real parents*?"

"Do they have any *children of their own*?"

"*Aren't they wonderful* to have taken that poor child in! I could never do that!"

During the adopted child's infancy his parents and extended family are getting used to the idea that adoption isn't respected by everyone as a first rate way to form families. They will use this time to grow used to such assaults and to educate others. They'll become more comfortable setting and keeping their own privacy boundaries. The child, then, becomes the beneficiary of this experience when his own questions arise later.

This is a time when adoptive families become comfortable saying the word *adopted* and begin to use it with their children casually. They may introduce their children to their personal arrival story and begin to use some early childhood books on adoption such *as A Mother for Choko* or *The Day We Met You* or *Tell Me Again about the Night I Was Born* or *Through Moon and Stars and Night Skies.*

Kids this age come to know the words—*adopted, birthmother*—and may even parrot them. But they don't get the concepts that underlie them. That will come gradually, through school years and into their teens.

At School

At pre-school or in kindergarten most adopted children are first exposed to others' negative bias about adoption. Having felt nothing but warmth and pride in their own adoption story, they share it with others, only to find that—particularly with some adults—the fact of their adoption seems startling or unsettling— perhaps even something to be ashamed of.

By the intermediate years of grade school, most adoptees are given the opportunity to come face-to-face with a frightening fact—in order for them to have been embraced by the loving parents and aunts and uncles and grandparents and cousins whom they love and call their own, some other family really did have to "lose" them or "give them away." Thus begins the ambivalent struggle to understand the "whys" of their adoption and to acknowledge and accept that as adopted people they have two very real families.

Children of this age are concrete thinkers, accepting themselves as responsible for everything that happens around them. Internally they will have lots of questions about why they were "given up." But some children are more vocal than others. They will have lots of questions and will ask them freely. Others say little about their adoptions. Sometimes their parents assume that this means that their children are comfortable with the information they have. More often, these children simply don't feel free to ask the questions they have—fearing that they will hurt their parents' feelings.

Sometimes grandparents are asked questions that parents don't hear. That being the case, it's important for extended family members to discuss ahead of time with the child's parents just what the parents would like them to do in such a situation. What calming and comforting and totally truthful information should they share before reassuringly referring these children back to their parents for the full scoop? Remember, you may not have been privy to the all of the details his parents have about this child. His story is *his story*, not the family's story, and so most of its details appropriately remain privately held between parent and child.

Adolescence

Adolescence is a time of testing the boundaries and preparing to "let go." For children who have been adopted, adolescence can be even more difficult. Their bodies are changing, yet unless the adoption is open, they may have no frame of reference for what to expect about their adult size and shape. Their fluctuating hormones and developing sexuality may lead some to fear that they will "repeat their birthparents' mistakes"—especially when, unfortunately, a parent or grandparent implies such. For those in non-open adoptions curiosity about birthfamily information often peaks during adolescence and they may begin to think about searching.

While all of this emotional turmoil is going on inside, most adolescents don't volunteer to talk with their parents about it. Unfortunately, this can lead them to get their support from poorly informed peers or others who have mostly myth and misinformation to share. Grandparents or favorite aunts and uncles who may be privileged to be called upon as listening ears need to be prepared to help and to share with the child's parents information they receive that the parents may need to know in order to help the child.

Adulthood

Marriage or expecting a baby is another trigger point for the interest in more information about one's birthfamily. More 20- and 30-something adoptees search than do teens or people in their middle age years.

📖 Learn more about it:

Flight of the Stork: What Children Think (and When) about Sex and Family Building by Anne Bernstein (Perspectives Press, Inc., 1994)

Raising Adopted Children by Lois Melina (HarperCollins, rev. 1998)

Real Parents, Real Children by Holly Van Gulden and Lisa Bartels-Rabb (Crossroad, 1993)

Telling the Truth to Your Adopted and Foster Children by Betsy Keefer and Jayne E. Schooler (Bergin & Garvey, 2000)

Talking to Young Children about Adoption by Mary Watkins and Susan Fisher (Yale University Press, 1993)

Making Sense of Adoption by Lois Melina (HarperCollins, 1989)

The Family of Adoption by Joyce Maguire Pavao (Beacon Press, 1998)

Being Adopted: The Lifelong Search for Self by David Brodzinsky, Marshall Shechter, and Robin Marantz Henig (Doubleday, 1992)

Voices from another Place: A Collection of Works from a Generation Born in Korea and Adopted to Other Countries edited by Susan Soon-Keum Cox (Yeong & Yeong Book Co, 1999)

Searching for a Past: The Adopted Adult's Unique Process of Finding Identity by Jayne Schooler (Pinon Press, 1995)

Expanding the Family Culture

Think about it. When your parents married they forged two cultures in which they were each raised into the one in which you were raised. If you parented with a partner, you did the same. Now your children are blending their own cultural heritage with that of children who joined them by adoption. The traditions, history, clothing, foods and more that are part of your beloved adoptee's heritage now become yours to explore and embrace. In exploring this new culture we may feel awkward at first, but, with familiarity, most of us in the melting pot cultures of the world have become adept at accepting new things as our own. In speaking English we speak a language whose vocabulary has been fed by more "foreign" languages than any other.

Family Heritage—Stories, Traditions, and Heirlooms

My own family is an interesting lot. We include people born to the family and adopted into the family and married into the family. We are of more than one race, Jews and Christians and agnostics. Despite our diversity, we share a very clear culture that is a melding of all of who we are and a sense that we all belong to each other—even on the days when we can't stand one another.

One "heirloom" we share among us is a cookie recipe that my husband Dave brought into my family from his own grandmother. Making those raisin-filled cookies is inconvenient. There's the dough, which must chill overnight. There's the filling, which must cook and then cool. There's the rolling and cutting and filling before the cookies must be iced. It's an all day job that begins the night before. We do this once a year—in December. Dave's family called these Christmas cookies. His grandmother made them, and after she couldn't, his mother made them. After she could not, I began making them, and I taught my own Grandmother, too.

My children consider making raisin-filled cookies a not-to-be-missed tradition that they have shared for the last 15 years with their other-side-of-the-family cousins (my sister's children) who happen to be Jewish. And so, one day in December a couple of adults and five or six of the cousins get together to make these cookies. Christmas carols and Chanukah tapes play in the background. We cut and ice the extra dough in the shapes of dreidels and menorahs and Christmas trees and reindeer. Then we pack these cookies into tins to share with Grandmas and Zeydies and uncles and aunts near and far—and of course with the daddies—the Christian daddy and the Jewish daddy who look forward to these special treats each year. The cookies are an heirloom passed from one generation to the next and then from one family extended to another.

I wish that there were no stories to share about heirlooms reserved only for "blood relatives" and wills that were written to exclude children not genetically connected to their grandparents. But there are, and they could fill a book. Some of the most poignant of these have been reported as the personal stories of some of adoption's most respected teachers and leaders. Most of these decisions were made out of ignorance and with little thought to what residual pain they might cause. The pain these exclusions cause goes far beyond the pain to the adopted children. Often the parents of these children feel even more cast aside and offended than do the adoptees themselves.

Furthermore, grandparents who have absolutely no intention of "leaving out" their adopted children should know that in some states probate law still presumes that adopted grandchildren cannot and should not inherit from their grandparents "as grandchildren" (after all, the grandparents did not choose to adopt—their children did). Unless these loved ones are specifically and individually named in their grandparents' wills and trusts they will not share in their cousins' or siblings' inheritance from grandparents. At the same time, these same laws prevent adopted people from inheriting from their birthrelatives, too. They are, in the law, "family-less."

Families, as we've said before, are connected by more than genes and blood. They are connected by love and by law and by social custom. Family trees include not just genograms, but are more social constructs, their twigs and branches made up of in-laws (and outlaws). Not only do you take on your expanded family's traditions, but you give them yours. Just as your mother-in-law's cookie recipes have become yours to share with friends at the holidays and your son-in-law's family's wonderful way of celebrating birthdays with a cake with a prize in the middle have now become something the larger family loves to do, I would hope that you would plan to share your heritage and history and traditions and heirlooms with *all* of your grandchildren, with *all* of your nieces and nephews and to hope that they bring some of the traditions of their own cultures into your family's culture.

📖 Learn more about it:

"Getting Real—Building a Sense of Entitlement" by
Patricia Irwin Johnston
http://www.adopting.org/pat_entitle.html

Adoption and the Jewish Family by Shelly Rosenberg
(Jewish Publication Society, 1998)

Understanding and Including Your Grandchild's Birthfamily

If the adoption in your family is going to be a fully open one, with extended birthfamily members from birthparents to half siblings to grandparents to cousins interacting on a regular basis with your family, you may understand the importance of learning more. But if your family's domestic or international adoption has been arranged with the expectation of full confidentiality—little background information, no identifying information, no visits or letters expected—you may be assuming that the birthfamily is a part of a past that can be put into a box on a closet shelf. Not true.

A core adoption truth is that every adopted person really, truly does have two families—one which birthed him and gave him many physical and emotional and intellectual characteristics and his genetic potential, and one which nurtured and loved and raised him, offering him his religion, a familiar culture of people and food and music and tradition, his religious training and his moral values—is difficult for everyone touched by adoption. Whether you know their names, write to them, shake their hands or not, your child's birthfamily will always be there. They will look back at you from his eyes, speak to you in the timbre of his voice, and make themselves known to you in his physical skills and limitations. They are a part of him and so will be a part of you.

As your beloved adoptee grows he is bound to have questions. Indeed, if he has been raised in a climate that values shared intimacy and respects inquiry, he will have a lot of questions. Most will be directed to his parents. Some will come to you. Earlier we discussed the importance of your learning to respect the privacy boundaries of this child's family in situations like this. But much of the conversation in which you might be engaged will be more general and wouldn't involve the need for intimate information. Chances are that your grandchild or niece or nephew will engage you in a conversation about adoption. How will you respond?

An important lesson of adulthood is that it is easier to deal with a difficult known entity than it is to deal with a mysterious unknown. Birthparents, adoptive parents, and their extended families have much to learn about what it means to be a birthparent or an adoptive parent or an adopted person, whether or not their relationships are to be communicative. The following books can help you to begin to educate yourself.

📖 Learn more about it:

The Family of Adoption by Joyce Maguire Pavao (Beacon Press, 1998)

Twenty Things Adopted Kids Wish Their Adoptive Parents Knew by Sherrie Eldridge (Dell Books, 1999)

Who Am I? And Other Questions of Adopted Kids (Plugged In) by Charlene Giannetti will illustrations by Larry Ross (Price, Stern Sloan, 1999)

Birthparent Grief by Brenda Romanchik (R-Squared Press, 1999)

I Wish for You a Beautiful Life: Letters from the Korean Birthmothers of Ae Ran Won to Their Children edited by Sara Dorow (Yeong & Yeong Book Co, 1998)

Shattered Dreams, Lonely Choices: Birthparents of Babies with Disabilities Talk about Adoption by Joanne Finnegan (Bergin & Garvey, 1993)

Out of the Shadows: Birthfathers Stories by Mary Martin Mason (Howard Publishing, 1995)

Reunion: A Year in Letters between a Birthmother and the Daughter She Couldn't Keep by Katie Hern and Ellen McGarry Carlson (Seal Press, 1999)

Special Issues

When You Were Adopted Yourself

It is possible that if you yourself were adopted this adoption may bring up questions and issues for you. It's important for you to be aware of this, because even if adoption has never been a "big deal" to you before, you may be surprised at the kinds of feelings that surface now. If your adoption was confidential and this one is open, you could feel both excited and enthusiastic or threatened or jealous. You cannot expect that your experience with adoption will be like this one. Each adoption is unique, and adoption in general has changed a great deal in one generation.

If you find yourself feeling anxious during the time of this adoption, consider taking the personal and private step of learning more about adoption today and exploring more deeply your own feelings about your own adoption.

📖 Learn more about it:

The Whole Life Adoption Book by Jayne Schooler (Pinon Press, 1996)

The Adoption Triangle (revised) by Annette Baran, Ruben Pannor and Arthur Sorosky (Corona Publications, 1994)

Bastard Nation is a "modern day" and (obviously) "in your face" adoptee support and advocacy group that sees access to records as a civil rights issue. The leadership is smart, innovative, assertive, and approaches this very serious situation with a wicked sense of humor. They can be found on the Internet at http://www.bastardnation.org

If You Were Adoptive Parents, Too

Boy, have things changed! Adoption is so different than it was for the parents of 30-year- old adults and older. How we talk to our children about adoption has changed. When and what we tell our children has changed. How we feel about and interact with birthfamilies has changed. There is more literature out there for both adults and for children than there has ever been and the Internet has connected adoptive families differently than ever before.

You will be able to be empathetic about the stresses and strains of the planning and waiting to adopt phases, and since parenting (whether by birth or adoption) is more the same than it is different across the generations, you will have much to offer. But don't expect that your experience will be "the same" or that it can even serve as the most effective model for this young family. Offer them your open-minded and full-hearted support.

📖 Learn more about it:

Adoption Nation by Adam Pertman (Simon and Shuster, 2000)

When Your Kids Are New Parents at "Grandparent Age"

These would-be parents may have waited a long time to consider parenting—until careers settled, until it was clear that there might be no parenting partner, until a second more successful marriage. You may well have assumed that, if not before now, there would never be grandchildren from this son or daughter. You may already have other grandchildren who are grown or nearly grown. You may have begun to imagine yourself as a great-grandparent. Your own experience as a more youthful parent may lead you to question the wisdom of parenting later in life.

Let me warn you that it is very difficult for childless folks who have taken up the quest for parenthood to be objective about the issue of their age. Age-related roadblocks may have been thrown in their way already—failed fertility treatments, agencies with age restrictions, a birthparent who "didn't want to place with people my parents' or grandparents' age," the cultural attitudes about age in some other countries. The truth is that even if your reservations are based in fact, there is likely to be absolutely nothing you can do to convince these folks that parenting possibilities have passed them by and they should be resigned to it.

You need instead to accept what is about to happen and to offer the kind of support you can. Here are some tips:

- While you yourself are healthy do all that you can to involve yourself with this grandchild. He may not have you with him for his high school graduation or his marriage, but the foundation of a wonderful relationship with grandparents is a gift beyond price. Visit and call frequently. Learn to use email. Look for ways to get the child care support you might need in order to have these very young children visit you.

- Plan for your own elder care in a way that does not burden your children, who will now have their hands filled with parenting young children when you may be in need of care or a little "special attention." Or, in a related future gift to these grandchildren, consider offering to fund (at premiums which will be quite low considering these parents' current ages) extended care insurance for your grandchildren's parents. That way, if these grandchildren find themselves worrying about care for aging parents at particularly young ages themselves, you will have removed a huge burden.

- If and when you do need more family care, or if you just want more family time, consider moving to be near this family rather than expecting that they will be able to find ways to visit you more frequently.

When This Is a Second Marriage

Are there birth children from the first? Are there stepchildren from the second? Will there be a "yours, a mine, and an ours" constellation? Complicated, yes, but the bottom line is that children can't have too many people to love them. You need not compete with other sets of grandparents, just join in, and do so with as much unconditional commitment as possible.

Foster Grandchildren

What if the new arrivals aren't "forever?" Some families choose to offer a special kind of love and support to children in need. They foster them. Though it is becoming increasingly common for families to use fostering as a route to adoption (they agree to foster children who *may*—or may not—become available for adoption), most foster families make this commitment knowing that their place in these children's lives is temporary. They also can offer them stability and love and a model for what functional family life can be, giving them a foundation to take with them and to build upon—whether they are going back to their birthfamilies or into adoption elsewhere. Foster families can help children deal with pain and loss and grow healthier themselves while their birthparents are doing the work they need to do to become their full time parents again. They can serve as the way station for infants or older children moving to adoption with another family.

Fostering is a special calling. By definition it is filled with the pain of loss. Not everyone can do it, but those who *do* need the respect and love of those who care about them.

And so do foster children. Though it may be painful to see him leave, what you should know about having been a foster child's extended family is that you will have made a big difference in the life of a child who becomes your foster-grandson, your foster-niece, whether for a few weeks or few months or even for years…if you just will.

📖 Learn more about it:

Fostering Families Today is a new magazine published by Louis and Company, Loveland, CO.
http://www.fosterfamiliestoday.com

Adoption and the Rest of the World

It's sad but true that most of those who have not been personally touched by adoption not only don't get it, but often don't respect the institution or those most directly affected by it—birthparents, adoptive parents, and people who were adopted. You may have been "one of them" once, but as you become "one of us" you may find yourself growing more and more sensitive to adoption issues and to that bias we've referred to as adoptism.

For example, where once you might not have thought twice about how small children see the adopt-an-animal program at your local zoo, when your own niece asks her mommy if it's true that she herself can be "traded in for another next year, just like Aunt Dot traded the giraffe for a penguin" you may feel your blood run cold. When your grandchild reveals his terror that, because he wets the bed and has trouble getting along with his brother, they might return him to the adoption agency like the puppy who bit and wouldn't be housebroken who was returned to the Humane Society you may stop dead in your tracks.

Since the 1980s Cabbage Patch doll craze the concept of adoption (and I'm talking about within the definition of its role in family building) has been used rather cavalierly in fundraising and marketing. You can adopt (complete with certification designed to look like a birth certification) anything from a median strip to a used videotape to a redwood. We don't joke this way with other terms related to family attachment. Does anyone suggest that you "marry" a nearly extinct whale in order to fund its salvation?

While on the one hand you may find it somewhat comforting to know about celebrities whose families are "just like ours"—Rosie O'Donnell, Steven Spielberg, Maury Povich and Connie Chung, etc.—you may also grow annoyed that their children seem to constantly bear labels ("She's their adopted daughter, Catherine") that "qualify" them as if they were "not quite real."

You can make a difference for the younger generation of your family if you're willing to take on this cause on any level—personal or public—and try to let others know how distressing this lack of respect can be.

📖 Learn more about it:

When Friends Ask about Adoption by Linda Bothun (Swan Publications, 1987)

Supporting an Adoption by Patricia Holmes (Our Child Press, 1984)

"Adopt-a Confusion: How Using Adoption to Catch Attention, Touch Heartstrings and Raise Big Bucks Exploits Children Who Were Adopted and Those Waiting For Permanency" by Pat Johnston
http://www.perspectivespress.com/pjadopta.html

Top Five Hot Buttons not to Push!
(or, Open Mouth, Extract Foot)

These are examples of amazingly insensitive comments heard recently by members of INCIID's Adoption Waiting Room Internet bulletin board. Names have been changed to protect both the guilty and the innocent. There are many people, who, before reading *Adoption Is a Family Affair!*, might not even have understood what was so bad about some of these comments, but you probably get it now. If you see yourself reflected or reported here, you may have some apologizing to do. If, on the other hand, you feel confident that you were never so insensitive, good for you! In that case, perhaps these examples will serve as an impetus for your helping to get the rest of your family circle better prepared for the addition adoption will bring to the family.

5. "What did it cost?" (Didn't your mother teach you it was bad manners to talk about money, politics and religion?)

- "From my mother-in-law when we first told her that we were going to adopt, 'You know, you can get a Mexican baby for $250!' "

- "Friends of mine adopted, and shortly after adopting the husband was telling a client about it and the client asked, 'Oh, well how much did she cost you?' No this was not a blundering idiot like most, but a social worker!"

- Q: "Why would you spend so much money on adoption after spending so much money on infertility treatment?" A: "Well, didn't you just buy that nice $35,000 SUV? This is *our family* we are talking about. Priceless!"

- "My brother-in-law told his kids that we were 'going to Korea to buy a baby!'"

- "Someone asked me if adopting babies from China was like a black market! I had to explain how they take good care of the babies and rigorously screen who they will allow to adopt and that the fee is used to keep the orphanages running and take care of all the kids, including those who won't be adopted. I sure don't ever want my kid getting the idea that she was bought on the black market."

- "An acquaintance who heard about our plans asked us 'How much will your child cost?' (ARGHHHHHHHHH) No further comment with this one. On the other hand, yes, my husband and I have had this question numerous times! Some people who have inquired are very sincere, as they too, are weighing the decision to continue infertility treatment, live childfree, or move to adoption. That is very understandable, and I respect that question from them."

4. "Adoption connections aren't real connections anyway!" (Do you really want to say "You can do better than this"?)

- "Are you sure you tried hard enough?" (to conceive)

- Q: "Does it bother you that they won't be your own?" A: "My favorite comment to this one is what I read from the INCIID Adoption Waiting Room bulletin board earlier this summer: 'I gave birth to them through my heart'".... that is the shorter version I use with this stupid question. It makes people think about how ignorant they were for asking in the first place."

- "I mentioned to my sister-in-law that I wanted to name my future adopted son Truman, nickname Tru. She said

'You can't call him Tru Kinglsey, because he is not a true Kingsley. He will not be related...umm, I mean by blood.' I was appalled and since then have refused to tell anyone the names I am considering for my future children."

• "My husband adopted his first wife's daughter at the age of 9 months (she is now 22) and adopted my son at the age of 3 (he is now 10)....much to our surprise, I am now 30 weeks pregnant. On New Years Day we went to husband's mother's house. His sister (whom he has never really liked and hadn't seen in over a year) comes swooping in the door and hugs him and loudly exclaims, 'I want to hug you before you get to become a *real* father.' My husband said very angrily, 'I've been a *real* father twice now, but thanks.' He was so angry, and I was so angry, especially because both his son and his daughter heard her comment. I couldn't believe how stupid and totally insensitive and wrong her comment was."

• Q: "What's her mother's name?"
A: "My name is Lisa."
Q: "No, I mean her *real* mother's name."
A: "I'm her mother."
Q: "NO, I mean her *real* mother."
A: "What do you think I am? Polyester?"
And then, as if I must be some sort of an idiot, I said, "Ohhhh you mean her birthmother!"
Q: Then she said, "Well you knew what I meant all the time."
A: "No I didn't. I'm her real mother and I always will be. What do you think Sara will go through if she heard u say that I'm not her real mother and she is too young to understand?"

• "From my brother who has a master's and a Ph.D. in theology when my mom told him over the phone that we were going to adopt: 'Why don't they just have their own kids?'"

- "Too bad you have to adopt...your real kids would have been real cute."

- Q: "What does her mom look like?"
  A: "You tell me; you are looking right at her!"
  Q: The nerve of this woman. She kept prying. She said "Come on you know what I mean."
  A: I said "No ,I do not!"

- "She looks like she could be yours!"

- "Can they get her back?"

- "What are you going to do when he's three or four and the birthparents want him back?"

- "Can you give him back if you find out he's retarded or something?"

- "An adult adoptee asked me, 'If you and your husband get divorced, will you have to give him back?' I was so dumbfounded I didn't respond how I really should have, which would have been to ask if *her* parents would have had to 'give her back' if they had ever divorced."

3. "Adopted people are 'flawed.'" (The Bad Seed myth or Racism)

- "My reproductive endocrinologist said, 'You might not want to adopt... you never know what you're going to get.' As if you know with a biological baby!"

- "Adopted kids are always so stupid!"

- "I was talking to my sister, who by the way, is very well educated and is currently in a high-paying, high-profile job... working for an AA man. I was mentioning to her about our long wait for our child. She (once again) asked what my 'criteria' was for our child... meaning, had we requested a newborn, toddler, what race..etc. I told her that all I asked for was that the child be under age 3. To which she said, with much surprise, 'Even a black child?' 'Yeeeeessss' I replied. 'But you don't know how to cook collard greens, or how to comb their hair!!... and Desiree (the daughter born to us) will KNOW that s/he is not her *real* sibling!!' she says, totally serious. Funny thing is, (and I also told her this) that I am hispanic (Colombian), yet I have NEVER cooked a Colombian meal for my daughter!"

• "I never knew Adopted Children could be so cute."

• "An old friend of the family said 'I think if someone is stupid enough to get pregnant and doesn't want the baby, she should turn around, walk the other way, and never look back.' I thought that was so cruel. As if he is so superior that he never has made a mistake, and as if a birthmother could ever forget her child. This experience taught me not to tell many people about our open adoption. It's really no one's business."

• "A co-worker of my husband said, 'I wouldn't adopt, you will never get a perfect child.' I was stunned when he told me. She has a toddler who I am sure isn't 'perfect' and I think anyone who expects any child to be 'perfect' is setting that child up for a life of misery!! My husband told her we were hoping not to have a perfect child, because it wasn't going to have perfect parents. GO husband!!"

• "When I told my friend (a woman who was aghast that there was another girl in her play group with the same name as her daughter—she wanted hers to be the only one with that name) that if I had a boy, I'd name him Noah she exclaimed 'Yikes! Why would you name him something so unusual, he's going to stand out enough as it is. Why not name him something normal, like Larry?'"

- Q: "Why don't you just try to get a healthy caucasian baby?" A: "HELLO!!!!! We want a baby from another country. That is our choice."

- Q: "Why on earth would you want to adopt a black baby. They are ugly, have kinky hair and are always boarder babies. No black baby is ever given up for adoption without drugs and alcohol. Could turn out to be a criminal, too."

- "Apparently, everyone born in Asia speaks an Asian language because it's a genetic thing. People are forever asking me if our toddler son Cameron (who was born in Vietnam)can speak English. Just for fun, I told one person he was bi-lingual. After all, he was just a baby and saying only *ma* which happens to be Vietnamese for *mother*) and *ba* (which is Vietnamese for grandmother). I suppose he's as bilingual as the next baby!"

- "Our Latina daughter was born in Alabama, but people are always asking me, 'Do you think she will have an accent?'"

- "Why not just adopt from Russia? At least they'd look like you?"

- "A girlfriend who told me during my infertility treatment, 'Why not just get a dog, it's a lot easier' (probably should have ended the friendship right then) noted the other night that 'It's a good thing you are adopting an Asian kid, because he'll be short like the two of you!' When I informed her that Koreans come in all different sizes like Americans she said, 'Well we all know that Asians are generally shorter than Americans.'"

- "I am 6' and my husband is 6'3" We have had two people tell us we shouldn't be adopting from Guatemala because our daughter will be short. Who cares!!"

- "Oh, no! You're going to adopt a *Mexican*?"

2. *"Didn't you know that..." (Ignorance isn't bliss in personal relationships)*

- "Why don't you just go and pick one out?" Gee, where's the closest Babies-R-Us store?

- "Will you tell her she's adopted?" Duh...our Chinese daughter and we won't exactly look alike.

- "We adopted our daughter from China in December, 1999. A few months ago we went out to dinner with my father- and mother-in-law. Our daughter was eating rice and get- ting it everywhere (she was 16 months old). My father-in- law said, 'If she were *home* she would know how to use chopsticks by now.' I just gave him a weird look and said, 'She is home, and what does chopsticks have to do with it?' I know he did not say it to be mean; he is just clueless. He loves his granddaughter to death."

- "If God intended for you to have children, you'd be preg- nant by now."

- "We are African American, and we have been asked more than once: 'What's taking you so long. Aren't there piles of AA babies that need homes? You must be doing some- thing wrong!' I think that her comment does kind of re- flect this notion that there are a lot of AA infants to be adopted — and this is in part supported by agencies and other adoption professionals. There isn't a 'surplus' of AA babies out there. What is closer to reality is that there are a lot of older children of color in the foster care system, many of whom are adoptable."

- "At Christmas my sister-in-law asked about the progress with the adoption, commenting that it is taking a long time. I told her our homestudy is being reviewed by the Immigration and Naturalization Service and this time frame is about what the agency projected. She responded,

'Well, if it doesn't work out you can always go for artificial insemination.' Was she really paying that little attention during all the years we struggled with infertility?????"

- Q: "Do you get to name her?" She was still a baby, and had only the name the Chinese government assigned to her. Should I have answered "No, I have to call her Rover for the rest of her life"?

- "Well, you should know adoption is expensive"...Hmmm., well thanks for telling us that. Those hours researching adoption must have done us no good.

- "You mean you can still adopt within the United States?"

And, last, but not least, Sad-but-True variations on the NUMBER ONE INSENSITIVE COMMENT TO THOSE WHO ARE ADOPTING—"Now you'll get pregnant! They always do."

- "'Adopt and then you'll get pregnant at last!' Does that mean the adoption won't have any meaning then if a woman becomes pregnant?"

- "Everybody in my life knows that my significant other is a woman and that we want to be mommies. So, when I told my oldest sister that we were planning on adopting, she delivered the usual line about getting pregnant now that we've decided to adopt! So I told her no, we've stopped all treatment. We're building our family through adoption. She insisted, 'Oh no, you won't need treatment. You'll get pregnant now that you are going to adopt.' I finally just said, 'Do you know how babies are made?'"

- "'Once you adopt you will soon become pregnant!' That is impossible since I had a complete hysterectomy. These people who say this to me, knowing I had the surgery, are down right mean. How cruel!"

- "My mother and my mother-in-law both really believe that once I adopt I'll get pregnant. In fact, I hear this from everyone I tell that I am trying to adopt. Sheesh, pregnancy after adopting only happens in about 5% of the cases and who knows what their fertility problem was."

- "My mother-in-law added the best comment to this one. 'If you adopt and get pregnant I am not coming to Ontario to help you with babysitting!' My response is 'THANK GOODNESS!'"

But it's not all bad. Marni checked in to report, "On the other side, I told one of my oldest/dearest friends (whose wife is thirty-two weeks along with their second baby) that I almost felt like I was pregnant. His comment? 'Well, you are an expecting mother.' Now, that's what I call a great comment."

You can redeem yourself and learn to be as sensitive as Marni's friend! What's more, you can help others "get it," too. Keep reading...

Recognizing Adoptism—Your Own and Others'

In their book *Inside Transracial Adoption* (Perspectives Press, Inc., 2000) which offers culture-sensitizing parenting strategies for inter-country or domestic adoptive families that don't "match," Beth Hall and Gail Steinberg discuss how our biases and prejudices color the way we adults interact with the world and how bias influences the way that children develop their senses of who they are. The following sections introduce a bias well-recognized in the adoption community, for which Steinberg and Hall coined the term *adoptism*. They have been borrowed with very few changes from pages 107-8 of *Inside Transracial Adoption* with the authors' permission.

Andrea, a birth mother, has moved on from her experience of placing her child for adoption, becoming a successful doctor and mother of two (more). She is a survivor who faced the worst choice she could imagine, and not only made the best choice she could, but lived through and with it. "People try to be there for me, they try to understand, but it's hard to hear the words that they offer because what's behind them, unsaid, is the way they really feel: Knowing I wasn't ready to be a parent.... Disappointing my family and friends, who *thought* they knew me.... Wanting my child to be with me but knowing I'm not the best choice.... Perhaps the hardest of all is to hear someone say, 'I think what you did was wonderful but I could never do it myself.' To be set apart is one of the hardest parts of being a birth mother. Not only did I lose my child, but I am judged as wrong, out of sync with the deepest laws of nature for making a choice that no 'real' parent, who truly loves her children, could make herself." Andrea gives words to a reality and pain that isn't often perceived, *even by those who may love us best. Parents who choose adoption for their children are considered not as good or as valid as parents who parent their children.*

Ben is an adult who was adopted at birth. He is now married, and he and his wife have a two-year-old who was born to them. They are hoping to adopt a second child. He told us this story: "I remember when I told my best friend that Lynn and I were planning to adopt. I couldn't believe his response. 'Why would you even think of that?' he said. 'You guys make great kids. Why would you want to take in someone else's cast-off without knowing what you're getting?' All I could think was, 'Wow! You know I'm adopted and that's what you say to me? What do you say about me when I'm out of the room?' Ben gives words to an incredulity many adopted adults have expressed: that others hold a hidden bias about adoption and that they never know when it will pop out and cause pain. *Even those who love them best may say something unexpected, summoning up the stereotype that* adopted *means reject, cast-off, bad seed, etc. People who are placed for adoption are not considered to have been as valued by their birth parents as children who are raised within their original families.*

We (Beth Hall and Gail Steinberg) met Sarah in the intimacy of a grief support meeting. Each person present had lost a child when a birth parent reclaimed custody. Three years before, Sarah and her husband had lost their son Greg (adopted at birth) when he was four months old. They had since adopted a little girl. Sarah spoke as a survivor, someone who had faced the worst she could have imagined and lived through it. "When Christine came and took away Greggie," she said, "people tried to be there for us. Everyone tried, but something always seemed off when they tried to comfort me. I just couldn't shake the feeling that underneath, even our closest friends secretly felt that her reclaiming him was somehow more right than his staying with us—right, according to some higher order of things. Feeling sorry for us was something separate. I know our friends and family did feel sorry for us, but something else was at risk, something no one ever talks about. I've come to think that most people, deep down, believe that birth mothers and children belong together—no matter what. Nobody ever said that to us straight out, but it was there. I think even the people who love us the best had those feelings, but nobody would ever come right out and say anything. Feeling set apart from everyone was one of the hardest parts of losing Greggie for me. Not only did I lose my baby, I was judged wrong—out of sync with the deepest laws of nature for wanting him when she had first rights." More than one pair of eyes welled up with tears. Sarah had given words to a hurt that isn't often spoken: *that even those who love us best may not regard our families formed by adoption as valid compared to families formed by birth—even those who love us best.* There was a long pause in the conversation after she spoke, as the hard truth sank in.

Racism:

A belief that race is the primary determinant of human traits and capacities.

A belief that racial differences produce an inherent superiority of a particular race.

Prejudice or discrimination against someone on the basis of race.

Sexism:

Prejudice or discrimination against someone on the basis of gender.

Adoptism:

A belief that forming a family by birth is superior to forming a family by adoption.

A belief that keeping a child with his/her biological parents is inherently better than is placing a child for adoption.

A belief that for those growing up as adopted people the primary determinant of human traits and capacities is genetics.

A belief that differences in family-building structures or methods produce an inherent superiority in families of a particular structure or method.

Prejudice or discrimination against members of the adoption triad.

The stories above are examples of adoptism at its core. Adoptism is a cultural belief that families formed by adoption are less truly connected than are birth families; that birth families should be preserved at all costs and under all circumstances except the most severely harmful; that people who were adopted were first rejected, maybe for a reason. No matter what place you hold in the adoption triad, such judgments and discriminations feel the same. As a society, we tend to understand the dangers of bias based on race, gender or class. *Adoptism is no different. Adoptism is just as damaging.*

And we absorb the biases of our society as we grow up. As with racism and all the other "isms," it's through recognizing our deepest attitudes that we can change those that must be changed. Perhaps society's belief that parents must stay with their children is linked to the dark fears of childhood: "What will happen to me without Mommy and Daddy? Who will take care of me?" Maybe some of the bias against adoption is an extension of the voice of that child who can imagine no means of survival but for parents to take care of children born to them.

Whatever adoptism's sources, the important thing is that we can change ourselves and our attitudes. Recognition allows forgiveness. We can forgive others because we share their fears. We can feel part of, instead of separate from, victims or survivors. Understanding the bias takes away its power.

Beth Hall and Gail Steinberg put the above section on adoptism so well in *Inside Transracial Adoption* that I can't imagine changing a word of it, can you? Now that you've read it, let's think about it a bit in the context of your family member's recent decision to adopt. "Isms"—prejudices and biases—become so firmly entrenched only when we are surrounded by a culture that supports those biases. When what we are taught by the culture that surrounds us—our parents and grandparents, the media, etc.—is that people of color are not "as good as" white people, or people of another ethnicity are inferior to our own ethnicity, or that women are not as capable as men, we come to believe it. Most of the time, the bias of "isms" is directed toward minority groups and is expressed by people who are in the majority. Moreover, sometimes we are absolutely unconscious about our own biases—most often because our own "privilege" as a member of the majority is so firmly entrenched that we take it for granted.

For many people, facing their own prejudices and biases comes as a real shock, often triggered by something very personal. For example, fathers of talented daughters often become ardent feminists as they watch their daughters struggle to be taken seriously. A white person who comes to love a person of color suddenly becomes painfully aware of the depth of racism and for the first time is cognizant of his own "white privilege."

Recognizing the bias against adoption—adoptism—is much like this. Adoption is far less common than is building a family by birth, and since most of us grow up in our genetic families of origin, we tend to know very little about adoption. When suddenly adoption becomes a part of our personal reality, our personal experience, our own family, we may, for the first time, become aware of how irrationally biased much of the world is against people who live adoption.

Adoption in the Media

Look around you. How frequently have you seen adoption covered fairly and accurately in the media? The news stories you read about adoption describe atypical situations most of the time. Think about it…

Tens of thousands of adoptions are finalized with little notice each year. Court cases involving a tug of war between birth and adoptive families are incredibly rare, yet most of us know most of the details of the stories of Baby Jessica, Baby Richard, Baby Jesse, "the Internet twins," and a handful of similar cases that made the headlines in the last decade or so.

The overwhelming majority of people who murder their parents were not adopted. Yet, most adoption experts will tell you that it is the rule, rather than the exception, for adoption to be mentioned in a local news story when an adoptee murders his parents. Similarly, most serial killers are not adoptees, yet, with some regularity, the media continues to lump together as if they were representative several famous serial killers who joined their families by adoption.

In addition to the adopt-a marketing schemes mentioned before, notice obituaries and family stories, especially of celebrities. Since we don't write descriptions such as "Mrs. Rooney is survived by two cesarean-section-born sons and a vaginally-delivered daughter," only the subtle second-best bias of adoptism can explain descriptions such as "President Reagan has four children: Patty, and Ron, Jr., with second wife, Nancy, and daughter Maureen and her adopted brother Michael, with his first wife, Jane Wyman."

Movies with an adoption theme are rarely realistic and are often exploitative or offensive—*Annie, Problem Child*, etc.

The pervasiveness of adoptism is the most logical explanation for your own initial fear and concern when your family member mentioned adopting. Now that adoption is to be a part of your own life, what can you do to fight adoptism—your own and others'?

📖 Learn more about it:

"Adopt-A Confusion: How Using Adoption to Catch Attention, Touch Heartstrings and Raise Big Bucks Exploits Children Who Were Adopted and Those Waiting for Permanency" by Patricia Irwin Johnston http://www.perspectivespress.com/pjadopta.html

Adoption Language

Understanding a bias usually creates an interest in helping others understand it and end it. One way to do that is to begin to model more sensitive and appropriate language. Respectful Adoption Language (RAL) is vocabulary about adoption which has been chosen to reflect maximum respect, dignity, responsibility and objectivity about the decisions made by birthparents and adoptive parents in discussing the family planning decisions they have made for children who have been adopted. First introduced by Minneapolis social worker Marietta Spencer as "positive adoption language" (PAL) or "constructive adoption language," the concept of respectful adoption language has evolved over the past 20-something years. The use of RAL helps to eliminate the emotional overcharging which reflects and perpetuate adoptism. The use of this vocabulary acknowledges those involved in adoption as thoughtful and responsible people, reassigns them authority and responsibility for their actions, and, by eliminating the emotionally-charged words which sometimes lead to a subconscious feeling of competition or conflict, helps to promote understanding among members of the adoption circle.

Chances are very good that part of your son's or daughter's preparation for adoption involved learning to use RAL. As they model it for you, they'll soon expect that you begin to learn to use it, too, for your grandchild's sake and for theirs. At first some elements of RAL may seem a bit stilted and awkward, but as you become more sensitive to adoptism and the impact it could have on your precious grandchild, niece or nephew, you will see its benefits, and your conversation will soon be peppered with RAL.

At the root of understanding the need for RAL is the very definition of family and what connects the members of various family groups to one another.

- **Blood and genes** (e.g. a birthmother and her birth daughter) relate some family members to one another.
- **Law** (e.g. a husband and wife) forges some family members' connections.
- Still other family members share no genetic ties or legal connections but are members of the same family by **social custom** (e.g. a man and his mother-in-law).
- Sometimes what binds together a group of people as members of the same family is neither genes nor law, but the **love** they feel for one another (a stepparent's mother, who serves as "Grandma," or a parent's close friend who becomes "Aunt Sally.")

Families expanded by adoption may not share genes, but they are connected by love, by social custom, and by law.

Still, the absence of a "blood tie" has often resulted in the unwillingness of some to acknowledge adoptive relationships as genuine and permanent. Think of the many examples we've discussed already.

As the concept of family changes most of us have begun to acknowledge that any two people who choose to spend their lives committed to one another are indeed a family. A couple who has chosen a childfree lifestyle and a single parent with children are just as much families as is a married couple who has given birth to six children.

Adoption is a method of joining a family, just as is birth. It is also a method of family planning used by some who feel they are unprepared to parent, just as are birth control pills or abortion. Adoption has an impact on the lives of those it touches, but it is not a "condition." It should not become a label.

In most situations not centering on adoption it is not appropriate to refer to the adoption at all. An exception may be in an arrival announcement, which is indeed adoption-centered. And when it is appropriate to refer to the fact of adoption, it is correct to use past tense—"Kathy was adopted," (referring to the way in which she arrived in her family). Phrasing it in the present tense—"Kathy is adopted"—labels Kathy with an implication that adoption is a disability with which to cope.

Similarly, when conscientiously using RAL, don't refer to a child as *one of your own*. This term implies that children are chattels. Children are not belongings, they are dependent human beings in need of long term care and guidance by parents prepared for the task.

Try to avoid such terms as *real parent, real mother, real father, real family*—terms which imply that adoptive relationships are artificial and tentative. Also avoid terms such as *natural parent* and *natural child*, which imply that in not being genetically linked we are less than whole or that our relationships are less important than are relationships by birth. Indeed in adoption, children will always have two absolutely "real" families: one by birth and one by adoption.

Those who raise and nurture a child are his *parents*: his *mother, father, mommy, daddy,* etc. Those who conceive and give birth to a child are his *birthparents*: his *birthmother* and *birthfather.* Technically, it would seem that all of us have birthparents, though not all of us live in the custody of our birthparents. But increasingly those who have chosen adoption for the children to whom they have given birth but are not parenting are asking that the terms *birthparent, birthmother,* and *birthfather* be used exclusively to describe those who have already made such a plan. For example, a pregnant woman dealing with an untimely pregnancy is not a birthparent. Before she gives birth, she is an expectant parent. Not until she gives birth and actually chooses adoption would she be appropriately called a birthparent.

In describing the decision-making process expectant parents go through in considering adoption as an option for an untimely pregnancy, it is preferred to use terms which acknowledge them to be responsible and in control of their own decisions. In the past, it is true, birthparents often had little choice about the outcome of an out-of-wedlock pregnancy. In earlier times they did indeed *surrender, relinquish, give up* and even sometimes *abandon* their children. In some countries, safe-place abandonment is the only legal way to choose adoption for a child. In North America, these emotion-laden terms, conjuring up images of babies torn from the arms of unwilling parents, are no longer valid except in those unusual cases in which a birthparent's rights are involuntarily terminated by court action—nearly always after abuse or neglect.

In an age of increasing acceptance of out-of-wedlock pregnancy and single parenthood, today's birthparents are generally well counseled and well informed about their options, and using Respectful Adoption Language acknowledges this reality.

Increasingly, as agencies take on the role of facilitator and mediator rather than lifter-of-burdens and grantor-of-children, the phrase *place for adoption* is also being questioned. In RAL, the preferred phrases to describe birthparents' adoption decisions are *make an adoption plan, plan an adoption* or *choose adoption* ("Linda chose adoption for her baby.") Well counseled birthparents who do not decide on adoption do not *keep their babies* (children are not possessions) but instead they *choose to parent them* or *make a commitment to parenting* ("After considering her options, Paula decided to parent her child herself.") .

The process by which families prepare themselves to become parents is often referred to as a *homestudy*. This term carries with it an old view of the process as a weeding out or judgment. Today, more and more agencies are coming to view their role as less God-like and more facilitative. The preferred term, then, is *parent preparation*, a process whereby agency and prospective adopters come to know one another and work toward expanding a family.

As both sets of parents consider the ways in which they may plan an adoption, their choices include retaining their privacy in a *confidential* (not *closed*) adoption or opting to have varying degrees of ongoing contact between birthparents and adopters in a process known as *openness in adoption*. Some adopters parent children born outside the U.S. in a style of adoption respectfully referred to as *international adoption*. The older term *foreign* has negative connotations in other uses and so is now discouraged. Similarly, adopters who choose to parent one or more older children, sibling groups, or children facing physical or emotional or mental challenges are said to be parenting *children with special needs* or *waiting children*. These terms are seen as potentially less damaging to the self-esteem of these children than is the older term *hard-to-place*.

While adoption is not a handicap, it is a life-long process. Frequently news stories refer to *reunions* between people who are related genetically but have not been raised in the same family. In most such instances these encounters do not carry with them the full spectrum of understanding that the usual use of the term *reunion* implies. While children adopted at an older age may indeed experience a reunion, most adoptees join their families as infants, and as such they have no common store of memories or experience such as are traditionally shared in a reunion. *Meeting* is the more objective way to describe the coming together of a person who has been adopted and the birthparents who planned his adoption. Additionally, *meeting* is a term which neither boosts unrealistic expectations for the event nor implies a competition for loyalties between birthparents and adoptive parents.

Respectful Adoption Language is serious business. Just as in advertising we choose our words carefully to portray a positive image of the product we endorse (selling Mustangs rather than Tortoises, New Yorkers rather than Podunkers), and in politics we take great care to use terminology seen positively by the class or group of people it describes, those of us who feel that adoption is a beautiful and healthy way to form a family and a responsible and respectable alternative to other forms of family planning, ask that you join us in considering the language you use very carefully when speaking about those of us who are touched by adoption! After all, you're about to be one of us!

📖 Learn more about it:

A web-based version of this section can be printed out for easy distribution to others at
http://www.perspectivespress.com/pjpal.html

Adoption Awareness Month

For over twenty years the adoption community (and you are now a part of that community!) has designated the month of November as Adoption Awareness Month. This special time provides an opportunity for enlightening others about a variety of adoption-related issues from the need for homes for waiting children to the need for legislation to enlightenment about adoptism and respectful language, and more. Of course making a difference in how people view adoption is welcome at any time, but during November you may find that there are ways that you can join local efforts by agencies, search and support groups, adoptive families organizations. You can as well do some things entirely on your own initiative.

The following is a sampling of things you could do on your own—during November or at any other time of the year—to make a difference in how adoption is understood.

- Call a birthmother you know and invite her to lunch. Show some compassion and let her talk about her feelings.

- Encourage would-be adopters you know to get all the information they possibly can about their child's birthfamily

- Attend any rally being sponsored in your area during Adoption Awareness Month (AAM). Even if it is being sponsored by a group you don't understand or find uncomfortable, you can learn a lot by listening with an open mind and engaging in dialogue.

- Take a list of your favorite adoption-related books for adults and for children to your local library. Use the catalog system to see whether or not your library shelves these titles. If not, suggest that they buy them, leaving your list of titles and authors (and publishers if you know them) with the collection specialists.

- Take somebody with you to an adoption conference. Help your extended family learn what they need to know about adoption.
- Take a social worker, facilitator, or adoption attorney to lunch!
- Offer your home to a family who may be traveling from their home elsewhere to adopt a child from your area. It will save them money on their travel expenses.
- Be a weekend foster home.

Feeling at a loss about where to begin at home? Perspectives Press, Inc. has a page from which the above list was excerpted called "Observing Adoption Awareness Month" at http://www.perspectivespress.com/adoptionawareness.html. Adoption.com has a calendar of daily suggestions for opening the subject of adoption to discussion in your family at http://www.adoption.com/contact/calendar.htm . The website of the North American Council on Adoptable Children (http://www.nacac.org) offers access to a packet of AAM materials.

You can make a difference!

How You Can Learn More

This small book has been peppered with section-appropriate "Learn more about it" sections referring you to books and web sites to help you with specific issues. Many readers may be interested in ongoing "continuing education" about adoption as a way that their family is expanding. There are many ways to do this.

Books, Newsletters, Magazines

Keep yourself up-to-date with the newest reading material by putting yourself on the mailing lists of the publisher of this book Perspectives Press, Inc.: The Infertility and Adoption Publisher (kind of a Simon and Shuster of the adoption niche) and Tapestry Books (PO Box 359, Ringoes, NJ 08551), a mail order catalog (with website at http://www.tapestrybooks.com) carrying the adoption-related books of dozens and dozens of publishers (making them kind of the Barnes & Noble or amazon.com of the adoption world).

You can be a lifetime learner by subscribing to one of the national periodicals on adoption. That way, every few weeks a small, easily digested piece of education between two covers will arrive just waiting to be curled up with. The two most expansive and inclusive are

Adoption Today (which now incorporates the older magazine *Roots & Wings*), a bimonthly publication of Louis and Company, whose publisher, Dick Fischer, is the father of daughters adopted from China. Call (888) 924-6736 to subscribe, or do so on-line at http://www.adoptinfo.net.

Adoptive Families (which now incorporates *Adopted Child*) is bimonthly publication of New Hope Communications, whose publisher, Susan Caughman is also the mother of a daughter adopted from China. Subscribe by phone at (800) 372-3300.

There are other newsletters and magazines with tighter foci— for example

Pact Press is the loosely scheduled publication from Pact An Adoption Alliance which deals with raising children of color who have been adopted. Their website is at http://www.pactadopt.org

PNPIC Post is a quarterly magazine from the Parent Network for the Post-Institutionalized Child at http://www.pnpic.org

Hoofbeats is the quarterly newsletter of the Attachment Disorder Network. At http://www.radzebra.org

The North American Council on Adoptable Children (a national advocacy organization for special needs adoption at http://www.nacac.org) publishes a quarterly newsletter called *Adoptalk*

There are dozens more.

Internet Sites

Some really great general interest adoption information can be found at these sites. They will have you surfing for days!

National Adoption Information Clearinghouse at
http://www.calib.com/naic

Adopt: Assistance Information Support at
http://www.adopting.org

Adopting.com, Internet Adoption Resources at
http://www.adopting.com

Support Groups

Throughout the country, support groups offer monthly meetings, newsletters, periodic seminars, telephone warm lines for families formed by adoption. They welcome the members of extended adoptive families—even when they are local to you but the adoptee lives in another city!

Some of these focus on a particular road to adoption or a special issue in adoption. Most of he specially focused groups below have chapters in many cities across the continent

FCC—Families with Children from China
http://www.fwcc.org

EEAC—Eastern European Adoption Coalition
http://www.eeac.org

FRUA—Families for Russian and Ukrainian Adoption
http://www.frua.org

Indian Adoption Information Support & Resource at
http://www.ichild.com

International Adoption Alliance http://www.i-a-a.org

PNPIC—Parent Network for the Post-Institutionalized Child http://www.pnpic.org

Stars of David—a support group for Jewish adoptive families http://www.starsofdavid.org

Adoption Council of Canada—the umbrella organization for local adoptive family support groups in Canada

Others are more general and include families built by all forms of adoption. You can find these local independent support groups by calling the North American Council on Adoptable Children at (651)644-3036 for a referral or by visiting Sandra Lenington's list of support groups in the Giant Directory of Adoption Resources at http://www.adopt-usa.org/resources/ Your membership in local adoptive family support groups is not contingent on your attending with the adopters! Everyone is welcome, so please consider affiliating with a local adoptive family support group even if your loved ones live in another city.

Conferences

Agencies or parent groups or coalitions of these often offer conferences open to the public in larger cities. Sometimes these are free and other times there is a reasonable fee charged. Extended family is always welcome at such conferences. In fact, conference planners would be thrilled to see you there (and some attendees will be envious that their own extended families have not come along).

Welcome to the world of adoption! You'll love it here!

About the Publisher

Perspectives Press, Inc.: The Infertility and Adoption Publisher

http://www.perspectivespress.com

Since 1982 Perspectives Press, Inc. has focused exclusively on infertility, adoption, and related reproductive health and child welfare issues. Our purpose is to promote understanding of these issues and to educate and sensitize those personally experiencing these life situations, professionals who work in these fields, and the public at large. Our titles are never duplicative or competitive with material already available through other publishers. We seek to find and to fill niches which are empty.

Currently in print titles from Perspectives Press, Inc. include

For Adults

Perspectives on a Grafted Tree
Understanding Infertility: Insights for Family and Friends
Sweet Grapes: How to Stop Being Infertile and Start Living
    Again
A Child's Journey through Placement
Adopting after Infertility
Flight of the Stork: What Children Think (and When)
    about Sex and Family Building
Taking Charge of Infertility
Looking Back, Looking Forward
Launching a Baby's Adoption
Toddler Adoption: The Weaver's Craft
Choosing Assisted Reproduction
PCOS: The Hidden Epidemic
Inside Transracial Adoption

For Children

The Mulberry Bird
Filling in the Blanks
Lucy's Feet
Two Birthdays for Beth
Let Me Explain

About the Author

Patricia Irwin Johnston (Pat) is the wife and sister-in-law of adopted people and the mom, through adoption, to three young adults, who in 2001 (the year of this book's publication) will be 17, 20 and 26.

She has been a prodigious award-winning volunteer within the infertility and adoption communities for over 25 years, serving on the boards of directors of several influential organizations. Currently she moderates discussion boards for Adopt: Assistance, Information Support and for INCIID and is a national advisor to INCIID and to Pact: An Adoption Alliance and to the new magazine *Fostering Families Today*.

Pat has written several books, including *Taking Charge of Infertility, Understanding Infertility: Insights for Family and Friends, Adopting after Infertility,* and *Launching a Baby's Adoption,* and her articles appear frequently in niche newsletters and magazines.

With a son grown and on his on and a daughter half way through college, Pat lives in Indianapolis in a rapidly emptying nest with her husband, her mom, and one nearly grown daughter. She's looking forward to grandparenting—by birth or by adoption.